ZUBAAN-PEN

SEEING LIKE A

Nivedita Menon teaches Political Thought at Jawaharlal Nehru University, Delhi. Her previous books include *Recovering Subversion: Feminist Politics Beyond the Law* (2004); an edited volume, *Sexualities* (2007); and *Power and Contestation: India after 1989* (2007, co-authored with Aditya Nigam). An active commentator on the blog kafila.org, she has also translated fiction and non-fiction from Hindi and Malayalam into English. She has been active with citizens' forums in Delhi on secularism, workers' and women's rights, sexuality, and in opposition to the nuclear bomb.

Praise for the Book

'Nivedita Menon combines a highly complex conceptualization of feminist theories and practices with a wonderfully engaging and perfectly lucid style of writing. She frames the debates within a rich understanding of larger socio-political processes, and reveals the interfaces between the two.'—Tanika Sarkar

NIVEDITA MENON

SEEING

LIKE A

FEMINIST

PENGUIN BOOKS

PENGUIN BOOKS

USA | Canada | UK | Ireland | Australia
New Zealand | India | South Africa | China

Penguin Books is part of the Penguin Random House group of companies
whose addresses can be found at global.penguinrandomhouse.com

Published by Penguin Random House India Pvt. Ltd
7th Floor, Infinity Tower C, DLF Cyber City,
Gurgaon 122 002, Haryana, India

Penguin
Random House
India

First published by Zubaan and Penguin Books India 2012

10 9 8 7 6 5 4 3

The views and opinions expressed in this book are the author's own and the facts
are as reported by her which have been verified to the extent possible, and the
publishers are not in any way liable for the same.

ISBN 9780143067429

Typeset in Minion by R. Ajith Kumar, New Delhi

Printed at Repro Knowledgecast Limited, India

www.penguin.co.in

CONTENTS

CONTENTS

INTRODUCTION

Have you heard of 'nude make-up'?

This is what it is:

'Nude make-up looks are all about your skin looking fresh and dewy, without looking like you're even wearing any make-up. All you need is eyeliner, mascara, nude lipstick, and a highlighting blush that will give your skin a natural-looking glow.'[1]

The whole point of nude make-up, clearly, is to spend hours painting your face in order to make it look like you had not touched it at all.

The maintaining of social order is rather like that. It requires the faithful performance of prescribed rituals over and over again throughout one's lifetime. Complex networks of cultural reproduction are dedicated to this sole purpose. But the ultimate goal of all this unceasing activity is to produce the effect of untouched naturalness.

When one 'sees' the world like a feminist though, with the gaze of a feminist, it's rather like activating the 'Reveal Formatting' function in Microsoft Word. It reveals the strenuous, complex formatting that goes on below the surface of what looked smooth and complete.

What do I mean by feminism? A feminist perspective recognizes that the hierarchical organizing of the world around gender is key to maintaining social order; that to live lives marked 'male' and 'female' is to live different realities. But simultaneously, to be a feminist is to imagine occupying the marginal, relatively powerless position with reference to *every* dominant framework that swallows up the space at the centre. For instance, any possible female reader of this book would be in a relatively powerful position with regard to the working-class men she interacts with daily—the auto rickshaw driver, the janitor, the domestic servant; and if she is an upper-caste Hindu in India, or a white American anywhere, with regard to men who are not. At the same time, she would experience her relative powerlessness *as* a woman if faced by a man in a position to attack her sexually, regardless of his class or caste; or when she compares her life choices and autonomy with those of a man of her class. Needless to say, it is not only 'women' who can adopt feminism as a political stance and way of life, but men who choose to do this have to take a stand against the privileges that they could otherwise take for granted.

Feminism is thus not about individual men and women, but about understanding the ways in which 'men' and 'women' are produced and inserted into patriarchies that differ according to time and place. My title is inspired by James Scott's *Seeing like a State,* but there is a crucial difference in the way 'seeing' operates in the two instances. Scott uses the metaphor of seeing to indicate the ways in which a modern state makes heterogeneous practices legible to itself in order to control them. Thus, the State's 'seeing' is invested with enormous power, because when it 'sees' an identity, it is making that identity 'real', its 'seeing' is simultaneously ordering society. On the contrary, when a feminist 'sees' from the position of marginality he or she has deliberately chosen to occupy, it is a gesture of subversion towards power; it disorganizes and disorders the settled field, resists homogenization, and opens up multiple possibilities rather than close them off.

To be a feminist is to understand that different identities—located hierarchically as *dominant* or *subordinate*—are produced at different times and in different spaces, but also to be aware particularly of the processes of gendering. By 'gendering', I mean the ways in which people are produced as 'proper' men and women through rules and regulations of different sorts; some of which we internalize, some which have to be violently enforced. To be a feminist is to recognize that, apart from gender-based injustice, there are multiple structural inequalities that underlie the social order, and to believe that change is possible, and to work for it at whichever level possible. Feminism is not an organization that one formally joins, and it can never be the isolated achievement of individual women. To be a feminist is to feel part of the history that has produced us; it is to insert oneself into two centuries of thick, textured narratives of struggles and celebrations that transcend national boundaries; to hear the strains of songs of anger and sorrow and militancy in many tongues; to remember our heroines, our foremothers; and, above all, to feel an enormous sense of continuing responsibility.

Is this book 'about India'? I think not. When we read Germaine Greer's *The Female Eunuch* or Simone de Beauvoir's *The Second Sex* or bell hooks' *Feminism is for Everybody* (I mention these iconic feminist texts in conjunction with mine in all humility, only because they would be familiar to many readers), we do not assume that they are writing 'about' Australia or France or the US. Rather, we see them as theorizing from their own location to make arguments about women and patriarchy in general, and while some of their arguments work in plural contexts, others do not. In this book, I draw on feminist scholarship and feminist politics in my part of the world to set up conversations with feminist debates and experiences globally. The key difference may be that, when we in the non-West theorize on the basis of our experiences, we rarely assume that these are generalizable everywhere. But we do believe that comparisons and engagements with other feminisms are not only possible, but unavoidable. Which is why, in this book, I often assume and address the lively global feminist voices that surround us. And when I say 'we', I generally mean feminists.

Let me reiterate, then, that my focus in this book is feminist politics and feminist ways of seeing the operation of gendered modes of power. So it is not about women in politics. In India today, the political scene is marked by fiery, independent, militant women—Medha Patkar in the struggle against ecologically unsustainable and unjust capitalist development; Irom Sharmila, force-fed under arrest for over eleven years by the Indian State, as she continues her fast for the repeal of the Armed Forces (Special Powers) Act, the law that enables her state of Manipur and the North-East of India in general to be treated as occupied territory; Mayawati, the

Dalit leader of one of the most powerful organizations of Dalits in India, the Bahujan Samaj Party—to name but three. On the other hand, there is active participation by women in Hindu right-wing and upper-caste anti-reservation politics, ecological movements and land struggles, as well as in armed Maoist movements. All these can be (and have been) studied from a feminist point of view, but that is not my project here because here, I limit myself to engaging only with ideas and activism that themselves directly address gendered modes of power today.

I would like to place here a contrary opinion to complicate the distinction I make between 'feminism' and 'women in movements'. Nalini Nayak, who works with fisher people's movements on issues of livelihood and ecological sustainability, terms ecological movements the 'resource base of our feminism'. She is suggesting that the two cannot be so neatly separated. Clearly, as feminists, we must engage politically with such movements, but only for the purposes of this one small book, I will maintain the conceptual distinction.

For the same reasons of space and clarity of argument, I do not go into the history of feminism in India, which goes back to the nineteenth century, and about which there is a large body of scholarship, to some of which you will find references at different points in the book. I have largely focused on the contemporary moment, addressing history only in order to show the process of emergence of features we see in the present.

My overall understanding of Indian politics is always part of the background, and has been more fully outlined in an earlier work co-written with Aditya Nigam, *Power and Contestation* (2007). There, we see the twin projects of the Indian élite, that of Nation and Capital, being militantly challenged and subverted by a variety of contestations, some of which are also in direct confrontation with one another. While that book, too, adopted a feminist lens to look at Indian politics, this book focuses directly on questions arising from the gendered nature of power.

This book is divided into six chapters that tackle what I see as key, interrelated themes. A quick note for the reader fortunate enough to have escaped stodgy academic training: the text is scattered with references to other books and articles, but these names and dates in brackets and the notes at the end may be skipped completely. They are there because I want to make it clear that my own argument emerges in conversation with feminist politics everywhere, and because some readers may want to follow up; but you can also let your eye filter them out, and you would still be fine. The details of all references in brackets in the text and in the endnotes are given at the end in an alphabetical list, and I have added five books as general references right at the beginning of that list.

In the end, I hope to have put in place, not answers, but new questions and new objects we had not seen before. To see like a feminist is not to stabilize, it is to destabilize. The more we understand, the more our horizons shift.

FAMILY

'If marriage is the end of life,
how can it also be the goal of life?'

THE STORY OF MONI

There is zero tolerance for those who breach the carefully produced 'natural' order of society by refusing to conform to norms of looks and behaviour. In a village in West Bengal, a few years ago, a young girl Moni was beaten, tonsured and stripped naked for dressing and 'behaving like a boy'. This outburst of violence reveals the effort that goes into maintaining the social order. It is all too easy to understand this incident as the action of uncivilized villagers, but how different would the response be in the very opposite of a remote village—say, in the head office of a multinational corporation—to a male employee who insisted on wearing a sari and bindi to work?

Thus, while the horror that Moni had to live through may be at the more extreme end of a spectrum, the point is precisely that social order displays—not the absolute presence or absence of intolerance to difference—but a spectrum of intolerance. Each of us bears responsibility to some degree for maintaining these protocols of intolerance, which could not be kept in place if every single one of us did not play our part. From bringing up children 'appropriately', to lovingly correcting or punishing their inappropriate behaviour, to making sure we never breach the protocols ourselves, to staring or sniggering at people who look different, to coercive psychiatric and medical intervention, to emotional blackmail, to physical violence—it's a range of slippages all the way that we seldom recognize.

But the violence Moni faced was not only about gender-appropriate looks and behaviour. It had another equally significant dimension—the anxiety around maintaining and protecting the institution of marriage. That is, of 'actually existing' marriage—the patriarchal, heterosexual kind. For the young girl was tortured not only because she behaved like a boy, but because she refused to give up her friendship with a newly-married woman of the village.

The question of gender-appropriate behaviour is thus inextricably linked to legitimate procreative sexuality. That is, sexuality strictly policed to ensure the purity and continuation of crucial identities, such as caste, race and religion. Non-heterosexual desire threatens the continuation of these identities since it is not biologically directly procreative; and if non-heterosexual people have children by other means, such as technological interventions or adoption, then the purity of these identities is under threat. Of course, even heterosexual, potentially procreative desire is seen as threatening when it refuses to flow in legitimate directions—hence the violence unleashed on those who fall in love with people of the wrong caste or religion.

The institution that manages this policing of sexuality is the patriarchal heterosexual family. The family as it exists is the core that sustains the social order.

This social order correctly recognizes that non-heterosexual desire and defiance of gendered appearance are, in fact, signals of a refusal to participate in the business of reproducing society with all its given identities intact. Moni was said to be sixteen, but she was so small and thin that she 'looks about twelve', according to a reporter who visited the village. How did she escape the binding force of those protocols that most of us seem to have internalized so unquestioningly? Evidently, the structure built by those protocols, which appears to be so 'natural', unquestionable and immutable, is shakier than it seems. There are fissures, there are leakages; its borders are porous and vulnerable. There are many, many more Monis, perhaps even inside ourselves. It is precisely because the structure is so fragile that such enormous force had to be mobilized against the recalcitrance of one thin little girl.

WHAT'S LOVE GOT TO DO WITH IT?

What is a family? A group of people who love and support one another over good times and bad? But just any group of people who do this are not recognized as a 'family'—for example, a group of friends, a homosexual couple with adopted children, unmarried mothers, women living with their siblings, and so on. 'Family' is an institution with a legal identity, and the State recognizes as a family, only a specific set of people related in a specific way. It is not only the law that defines 'family'—extra-legally too, you are forced into being part of a family which is strictly defined in this narrow way. Many housing societies, for instance, have an informal understanding that they will allow only married heterosexual couples as tenants. A 'family' can only be a patriarchal, heterosexual family: a man, his wife, 'his' children.

In 1984, a judgment of the Delhi High Court said that the Fundamental Rights ensured to every Indian citizen by the Constitution, were not applicable in the family: these rights have to stop at the door of the home. Letting Fundamental Rights into the family, said the judge, would be 'like letting a bull into a china shop.'[1] The judge was, in fact, absolutely right. If you bring Fundamental Rights into a family, and if every individual in the family is treated as a free and equal citizen, that family will collapse. Because the family, as it exists, is based on clearly-established hierarchies of gender and age, with gender trumping age; that is, an adult male is generally more powerful than an older female.

Thus the family, as an institution, is based on inequality; its function is to perpetuate particular forms of private property ownership and lineage—that is, patrilineal forms of property and descent, where property and the family 'name' flow from father to sons.

I remember this lovely moment in the Hindi film *Mrityudand* in which the characters played by the actors Shabana Azmi and Madhuri Dixit are married to two brothers. Shabana's husband is impotent and everyone in the village knows it. She goes away for a while and has an affair; when she comes back home, she is visibly pregnant. Her sister-in-law Madhuri Dixit asks her in shock, '*Didi, yeh kiska bachha hai?*' (Whose child is this?) Now, this question is absurd and unnecessary because clearly, the baby is inside her body, it is hers; but the absurd question makes absolute sense in a patriarchal society (and only in a patriarchal society)—who is the father of this child, is the question. Whose caste does this child bear, to whose property can he lay claim?

Shabana answers simply, '*Mera*'. (Mine). I remember the hushed buzz at this reply among the audience in the theatre, some giggles. Some anxiety?

The fact is, no man can ever know whether a child is his. A woman knows a child is hers, but a man can never know whether it is his, not even with a DNA test. A DNA test can only tell you if the child is *not* yours, but if your DNA matches, it only indicates 'a high statistical probability' that it is your child. As they say, 'Motherhood is a biological fact, fatherhood is a sociological fiction.' It is this knowledge that creates permanent anxiety for patriarchy, an anxiety that requires women's sexuality to be strictly policed.

The furore around Valentine's Day is revealing of the perceived threats inherent in undisciplined 'love'. In India, Valentine's Day has come to be increasingly popular since the 1990s. As feminists, we didn't particularly approve of Valentine's Day, because we have a critique of this narrative about 'romance', where only one kind of love story is a real love story. Of course, it must be a man–woman story, and of course, even when you 'fall in love', more often than not, you end up 'falling for' an appropriate person—the man at least a few months older than the woman, at least two inches taller and earning at least a little more than her! The whole point about 'romance' is that the woman is somehow always smaller, more diminutive in a cute sort of way, while the man is adult. So, we feminists have long had a critique of 'romance' which is supposed to be so uncontrollable, but which ends up being so appropriate to patriarchy.

We also have a critique of Valentine's Day because it is less about 'love' and more about buying and selling and the market—because, on Valentine's Day, it is not enough to love someone, you have to buy something to prove it—cards, flowers, teddy bears. When the phenomenon began to manifest itself in the liberalizing 1990s, we were critical of it because it seemed to be the perfect example of the new consumerism.

But very soon, the Hindu Right began to attack Valentine's Day as dangerous to 'Indian values'; not just verbally, but also carrying out physical attacks on couples courting in public. This attack on Valentine's Day coincided with increasing instances all over the country—including big cities—of families violently separating couples who chose to marry outside their caste or religious community, often killing one or both of them. Such murders have come to be dubbed 'honour killings' by the English media, but a starker, more revealing term is suggested by Pratiksha Baxi—'custodial deaths', since the young people killed in such cases are in the custody, much like prisoners, of their own families.[2] We saw the link too, to increasing instances of 'lesbian suicides', that is, women who committed suicide, leaving letters saying that they loved particular women without whom they could not live, but from whom they were being separated by their families. Each such instance of violence that reaches public attention makes visible the growing challenge to the caste and community norms of sexual propriety.

B.R. Ambedkar had seen the potential of inter-caste marriage for what he called 'the annihilation of caste'. In a famous passage first published in 1936, he said: 'Where society is already well-knit by other ties, marriage is an ordinary incident of life. But where society is cut asunder, marriage as a binding force becomes a matter of urgent necessity. *The real remedy for breaking caste is inter-marriage. Nothing else will serve as the solvent of caste'* (Ambedkar 1936: 67).

Evidently, Ambedkar's recognition of inter-caste marriage as being potentially disruptive of caste identities is one that continues to be shared—and feared—by caste panchayats seventy-five years later. As feminists, though, we might like to discount the healing power of marriage as a 'binding force' in this process, for reasons that will be made clear as we go along.

In the second decade of the twenty-first century, the term 'honour killings' has come to be routinely used in the context of the traditional multi-clan village councils of the Jat community in Haryana, the *khap panchayats,* which have ordered and carried out murders of couples who choose 'inappropriate' marriage partners. These distinguish themselves from the *sarkari* panchayats instituted under the State umbrella, and claim greater legitimacy with the community, which may well be true. The *khap panchayats* have been demanding amendments to the Hindu Marriage Act to ban marriages that are *sagotra* (within the same patrilineal clan or *gotra*) and *bhaichara* (within the same circle of villages). Along with social pressures against inter-caste marriage, these combined restrictions would effectively ensure that almost everybody in the immediate vicinity of young people growing into adulthood would be taboo for romance—those of the same caste too closely related and those not related, of the wrong caste—thus leaving marriage decisions firmly in the hands of the family.

It has been argued that the urban English-educated élite with nothing but contempt for villagers are responsible for the image of *khap panchayats* as violent and dictatorial, whereas the communities they govern are content with them. However, it is important to note that the challenge to the authority of the *khaps* after all, first arises from the young people *within* these communities. Indeed, the issue has come to the notice of the 'urban élite' only because of the deep resistance to the diktats of the *khap panchayats* from the young people of these communities, who risk social boycott and even death for love.*

In short, feminists recognize what conservative forces in India see as dangerous in Valentine's Day. The subversive potential of love. Love that refuses to be tamed within the rules of caste and community and heterosexuality.

THE SEXUAL DIVISION OF LABOUR

But let's face it, once that love has been nicely fitted into the institution of marriage, it's a marriage like any other. Friends and I have often swapped stories of the bizarre experience of *defending* arranged marriage in the face of naïve well-meaning people from Western cultures asking in horrified tones: Do you still have arranged marriage in India? Marriage is marriage, we find ourselves saying. How many in the West 'fall in love'—helplessly, it is implied, as opposed to the rigid control of the arranged marriage—with someone whom their parents would not have found for them? And how

---

* Ah, here I suspend my cynical observations on love and romance!

different is the conduct of the actual marriage eventually?

One of the key features of this institution is the sexual division of labour. Women are responsible for housework; that is, for the reproduction of labour power. The labour that goes into making people capable of working day after day (food, clean homes, clean clothes, rest) is provided by women. The woman of the house is expected either to perform these tasks herself, or be responsible for ensuring that a low-paid poorer woman does it. In either case, domestic work is considered to be women's primary responsibility even if, as is most often the case, they are also performing labour outside the home and earning wages, or a salary.

There is nothing 'natural' about the sexual division of labour. The fact that men and women perform different kinds of work, both within the family and outside, has little to do with biology. Only the actual process of pregnancy is biological, all the other work within the home that women must do—cooking, cleaning, looking after children, and so on (the whole range of work which we may call 'domestic labour')—can equally well be done by men. But this work is considered to be 'women's work'. This sexual division of labour extends even to the 'public' arena of paid work and, again, this has nothing to do with 'sex' (biology) and everything to do with 'gender' (culture). Certain kinds of work are considered to be 'women's work', and other kinds, men's; but more important is the fact that whatever work women do, gets lower wages and is less valued. For example, nursing and teaching (particularly at lower levels) are predominantly female professions and are also comparatively ill-paid in relation to other white-collar jobs which the middle classes take up. Feminists point out that this 'feminization' of teaching and nursing is because such work is seen as an extension of the nurturing work that women do within the home.

At the same time, once 'women's work' is professionalized, there is practically a monopoly on it by men. For instance, professional chefs are still largely men, whether in New Delhi or New York. The reason is clear—the sexual division of labour ensures that women will always end up having to prioritize unpaid domestic work over paid work.

The fact is that it is not a 'natural' biological difference that lies behind the sexual division of labour, but certain ideological assumptions. So, on the one hand, women are supposed to be physically weak and unfit for heavy manual labour but both in the home and outside, they do the heaviest work—carrying heavy loads of water and firewood, grinding corn, transplanting paddy, carrying head loads in mining and construction work. But at the same time, when the manual work that women do is mechanized, making it both lighter and better-paid, then it is the men who receive training to use the new machinery, and women are edged out. This happens not only in factories, but even with work that was traditionally done by women within the community; for example, when electrically-operated flour mills replace hand-pounding of grain, or machine-made nylon fishing nets replace the nets traditionally hand-made by women, it is men who are trained to take over these jobs, and women are forced to move into even lower-paid and more arduous manual work.

The Equal Remuneration Act was passed in 1976, but women are routinely paid less than men for the same work.

One of the ways in which contractors/employers get away with this legally, is by segregating men and women into different parts of the labour process, and then paying less for the work that women do. The claim is that it is not 'women' being paid less than 'men', but the work that is lower paid, even though the work would be no less physically strenuous or skilled than the work given to men.

The unpaid work that women perform includes collection of fuel, fodder and water; animal husbandry, post-harvest processing, livestock maintenance, kitchen gardening and raising poultry that augment family resources. If women did not do this work, these goods would have to be purchased from the market, services hired for a wage, else the family would have to do without. However, so naturalized are assumptions about gender roles that the Indian census did not recognize this as 'work' for a long time, since it is not performed for a wage, but is unpaid labour around the family. Women themselves tend not to report such work because they see it as 'domestic' responsibilities. Even when their activities generate income, they may get ignored if they get wedged in between other domestic chores (Krishna Raj 1990; Krishna Raj and Patel 1982). Women's work thus remained invisible. As a result of sustained pressure from feminist economists, in the 1991 census, for the first time, the question, 'Did you work at all last year?' was amended. To it, was added the phrase, 'including unpaid work on family farm or family enterprise', thus enabling such work to be made visible to the State. Feminist interventions that have made such changes possible believe that the more accurate the information the State has on the kinds of work performed by women, the more fine-tuned its policies on poverty reduction, employment generation and so on, are likely to be.

The sexual division of labour has serious implications for the role of women as citizens, because every woman's horizons are limited by this supposedly 'primary' responsibility. Whether in their choice of career, or their ability to participate in politics (trade unions, elections), women learn when very young, to limit their ambitions. This self-limitation is what produces the so-called 'glass ceiling', the level above which professional women rarely rise; or the 'mommy track', the slower career track upwards, while women put aside some of the most productive years of their lives in order to look after children. The assumption that women's primary profession is motherhood drives state policy as well—the governments of France, Germany and Hungary give women three years of maternity leave, in the hope of boosting the birth rate. In 2008, the Indian government increased maternity leave for its employees to six months, besides instituting paid leave to its female employees for a further two years (to be availed of at any time) to take care of minor children. This measure, reported a newspaper, would 'turn women in India Inc. green with envy.' That is, women employees in the private sector would kill to have the same privilege which women in government employment have—the privilege of compromising their career advancement. It is hard to remember in the midst of all this that children have two parents most of the time, that child-rearing is not the job of one parent alone. A single mother should not have to take the difficult decision of putting her career on the back-burner to bring up children, while younger men race ahead of her because their childcare responsibilities are fully borne by their wives.

The point is not that housework and child-rearing are meaningless and dull, but rather, that both the positive and creative aspects of this work as well as the drudgery of it, should be shared equally by men and women.

The sex-based segregation of labour is the key, to maintaining not only the family, but also the economy, because the economy would collapse like a house of cards if this unpaid domestic labour had to be paid for by somebody, either by the husband or the employer. Consider this: the employer pays the employee for his or her labour in the workplace. But the fact that he or she can come back to the workplace, the next day, depends on somebody else (or herself) doing a whole lot of work the employer does not pay for—cooking, cleaning, running the home. When you have an entire structure of unpaid labour buttressing the economy, then the sexual division of labour cannot be considered to be domestic and private; it is what keeps the economy going. If tomorrow, every woman demanded to be paid for this work that she does, either the husband would have to pay her, or the employer would have to pay the husband. The economy would fall apart. This entire system functions on the assumption that women do housework for love.*

At one moment in the history of feminism, there was a move for demanding wages for housework. In the UK in the 1970s, this was a powerful rhetorical tool, because it forced recognition of the fact that the domestic work

---

* And is it only in tennis that 'love' means nothing?

which women do has economic value. But many feminists feel that this demand leaves untouched the sexual division of labour—indeed, measures like paid maternity leave for three years, can be seen as a form of 'wages for motherhood' but, as we have seen, it fixes women more rigidly into work defined as 'women's work'.

In 2010, a significant judgement by the Supreme Court in India pronounced on the value of the domestic work carried out by women. A homemaker died in a motor accident, and her husband claimed compensation. A tribunal awarded him an amount, calculating an unemployed wife's income as a third of the husband's income. The husband appealed in the Supreme Court, seeking an enhancement in the amount. In its judgement, the Supreme Court increased the amount considerably, and further held that to see women's home-based work as being without economic value, displayed gender bias. The judges suggested that not only the particular law in question (the Motor Vehicles Act) but also other laws should be changed, and the question of the value of women's work should be taken up by Parliament (Gunu 2010).

It is important to remember the context of this landmark judgement on the value of women's domestic work. It was occasioned by the death of a wife and addressed the question of monetary compensation to the husband's family for the loss of the person who had performed that work. Is it possible to conceive of a judgement of this kind if a living woman had gone to court seeking financial recompense for her labour from her husband? I have my doubts. However, even if she had, like some other feminists during the wages-for-housework movement, I would have my misgivings about the re-privatization of the sexual division of labour, so that the husband becomes the wage-payer and the woman the worker.

Domestic work has an inescapable, but invisible, social dimension that must be recognized. This dimension becomes visible only when we consider those who do perform this labour for a wage—domestic 'servants'.

DOMESTIC SERVANTS

One estimate of the number of domestic workers ('servants') in India is made on the basis of the fact that the white-collared middle class in India is around three crores. Assuming most of these would have a maid, and that some would be in the same family, the number of domestic workers is likely to be more than 1.5 crores.

Consider now the following information. In the first all-India survey of non-unionized female sex workers conducted recently, 71 per cent said they had moved voluntarily to sex work after having found other kinds of work to be more arduous and ill-paid. The largest category of prior work was that of domestic workers. In other words, a large number of women in the sample had found being a domestic servant to be more demeaning, exhausting and ill-paid than sex work (Sahni and Shankar 2011). For the middle-class employers of 'maids', in whose imagination becoming a prostitute is a fate worse than death, this fact should produce an utterly shaming moment of self-reflection.

There's nothing inherently demeaning about cleaning up other people's homes or cooking for them for a wage; it could be just another job. But not in India. Here the work has the worst aspects of both feudalism and capitalism.

The callousness of the Indian middle classes towards their 'servants' outdoes the worst excesses of feudalism. The polite term 'domestic help' that has replaced the word 'servant' in public usage is perniciously misleading. Make no mistake— these are servants. They are treated as less than human, less than pet animals. Apart from facing physical and sexual abuse—which is common—domestic workers perform heavy unrelenting toil, for they have no specific work hours if live-in; no days off or yearly vacations if part-time.

Not to mention the routine humiliation that is their due. Several times now, I have noticed in Delhi restaurants the truly appalling sight of young women who are clearly maids in charge of toddlers, standing throughout the meal that their employers are consuming, ready to take charge of the baby at any point, and not being offered so much as a glass of water. One such young trendy couple I saw could easily have been students in the US where, if they ever undertook babysitting to meet their expenses, they would expect to be treated with dignity as employees, nothing less. This disdain towards those who perform essential manual labour is deeply casteist and a fundamental part of the psyche of the upper-caste Indian middle classes, whose 'progressive' credentials are often displayed exclusively in permitting the Dalit sweeper to enter the kitchen to wash their dirty dishes!

Formerly, the feudal family servant could at least expect to be broadly looked after in times of need, but the modern servant can at best expect small loans for personal emergencies, to be deducted from the pittance they are paid. On the other hand, a capitalist work contract could be more dignified than a feudal situation—two parties mutually deciding terms and conditions. It can also be more alienating than the generations-old feudal bond, with no human relationship beyond the lines of the contract but, at least in principle, it is more equal. The Indian servant knows neither the safety net of the feudal servitor nor the formal equality of the capitalist contract; at the same time he or she bears both the humiliation of the feudal hierarchy and the cold exploitation of capitalism.

The isolation faced by young live-in maids is terrifying—they arrive from distant places to big cities like Delhi and Mumbai, often do not know the local language, are restricted to the houses in which they work, the only human interaction they have, being with their employers who are away all day—if that interaction can be called 'human' in most cases. Only where church agencies are involved is there some supervision of employers' treatment of maids.

The crisis for the middle classes in many Indian cities, and in states like Kerala with better-paid work in other sectors, is that domestic servants have become hard to come by. Domestic labour has become the least preferred option among manual labour jobs. Hence, perhaps, the recent spate of articles in English-language journals holding forth in witty pieces and interview-based articles, on the eccentricities of individual maids; the difficulties of finding a 'good' maid or nanny; the fact that it has become a 'sellers' market.' Revealingly, we never find interviews with maids themselves. There might be a photograph of a maid on her knees, swabbing the floor; or in a cute saucy cartoon, waving her broom, but what does she have to say? We don't know.

One extraordinary voice of a woman domestic worker to which we do have access is the autobiography of Baby Halder, originally written in Bangla and then translated into several languages including English, as *A Life Less Ordinary* (2006). It is a simple, unsentimental telling of a life of stark poverty and then exploitation by a series of employers, until she came to work for the retired professor who encouraged her to write. We need many more such voices out in the public realm, so that the complacency of the Indian middle classes can be shattered.

Some other people missing in those articles about servants that I mentioned above—the middle-class men. The usual interviewees are people called 'working women'—that is, they are paid to work outside the home. And because they do, they cannot perform their real work of looking after the home and children without pay. So they must pay other women (and sometimes men) to do this work that they would themselves have done for free. But their husbands, the fathers of all those children, have nothing to do with all of this—*they* have a life to get on with. And so the heartbreaking stories from women— I had to ask the driver to babysit because I couldn't miss an important meeting, I had to miss an important meeting because the nanny didn't turn up. Meanwhile, the bearers of sperm never miss a meeting—however trivial.

Then you suddenly also understand why employers don't want to hire women (except to look after their children)— they're always having servant problems. It is women, not men, who are assumed to be the employers of 'servants'.

Recently, two successful corporate women wrote newspaper columns about the need to treat maids as employees, pay them well, treat them with dignity, give them the perks and amenities you yourself would expect as an employee. If you don't do this—they warn women—be prepared to be less than efficient at your own job. Because your husband isn't ever going to get involved (Bijapurkar 2011; Kalra 2011). Basically, the ill-paid labour of domestic servants mitigates the intra-couple conflict that could be generated by the unfair sexual division of labour.

If this is the case, then the salary paid to any male employee actually includes a hidden element—the cost of this labour; whether paid for, or performed free by the wife. For that employee could not go back to work every day if this labour remained undone. And there would be no one to work at all in the long run if no children were being brought into adulthood. It's the argument feminists have made for a long time—if women stopped performing this unpaid labour, or taking responsibility for its being performed, economic systems would come to a grinding halt. It is the unpaid labour of women on which the economy is based.

There are several private and church-run agencies that regulate the supply of domestic help, the former run for profit, the latter not. Private agencies tend to prioritize the needs of the middle class for 'safety' and 'training' rather than the interests of the workers; while Church-run agencies lay down a few minimum conditions of work, like a weekly day off. More significant is the emergence, over the late 1980s to the present, of trade unions of domestic workers in several parts of the country, including Bengaluru, Pune and Delhi, which have tried to exert pressure on state and

Central governments to bring about legislation regulating their wages and work conditions. At a convention in 2011, the International Labour Organization (ILO) decided to adopt a set of international standards to improve the working conditions of domestic workers worldwide. In the wake of this, the Karnataka government passed legislation fixing minimum wages for domestic workers. The National Advisory Council (NAC) came up with a suggestion to bring domestic servants, both part-time and live-in, under the purview of the Minimum Wages Act and other labour regulations, such as an eight-hour working day, paid leave and maternity benefits. This is a welcome initiative, although the implementation mechanism is not clear.

However, these kinds of initiatives still locate the work of child care within the individual home, and still leave the maid at the mercy of the individual employer. Why not have legislation that makes day care for children the responsibility of every employing institution? Then the child-minders would be employees of the company or of the government the way the parents are; it would generate employment, increase productivity; the children would be safely close to their parents. Of course, feminists would then have to ask a further question—what about the children of the child-minders and maids? In other words, there would have to be expanding networks of child care—this is a social responsibility, and should not be the responsibility of individual women nor even of the family alone.[3]

CHANGING FORMS OF THE 'HINDU' FAMILY

We need to recognize that this form of the family—nuclear, patriarchal and patrilineal (that is, descent traced through males, and property inherited through males)—is not natural, nor is it something that has always existed in all parts of India. In this section, we take as an illustration, the emergence of the current form of the 'Hindu' family, which is based on an upper-caste North Indian norm. A key feature of this form of marriage and family is patrilineal virilocality, in which the woman has no rights in her natal home (the home into which she was born) and leaves it forever after marriage, moving to her husband's home, with limited rights as a wife.[4] But other forms of the family have existed till well into the twentieth century. For instance, in the Nair community of Kerala that I come from, until my grandmother's generation we were matrilineal. A normal household (*tharavaadu*) for my grandmother meant sisters and brothers living with the sisters' children, and these children's fathers would continue to live with their own sisters. It sounds odd today, but it was perfectly 'natural' to them. This form of family was legally ended in the late nineteenth century through interventions brought about by the British in partnership with the Nair male élite (Arunima 2003; Kodoth 2001). However, even as late as the 1970s, its vestiges remained.

The point is that the family we think of as natural is only one kind of family. Even today, in Meghalaya, amongst the Khasis, there is a form of matriliny where the youngest daughter inherits the property. She lives with her parents to look after them in their old age, and her husband joins her in that house. I watched a TV programme in which a Khasi woman said this, and the studio audience, all Delhi-ites, burst into derisive laughter. There is no sense amongst most of us that there are heterogeneous practices in this land mass we call India, and that there are many ways in which people can love each other, live with each other, be with each other.

There have been many and varied forms of the family among the many communities that came to be called 'Hindu', but gradually, from the eighteenth century onwards, through a strange partnership of British colonialism and the male nationalist élite, all forms of family and property arrangements that did not match Victorian and upper-caste Hindu norms of 'modernity' were gradually delegitimized.

The colonial government, in consultation with self-styled community leaders, organized vastly heterogeneous family and property arrangements within the ambit of four religious personal laws—Hindu, Muslim, Christian and Parsi. These personal laws which are being today defended by self-styled community leaders in the name of tradition and religious freedom, are colonial constructions of the nineteenth and twentieth centuries. Even the very identities of Hindu and Muslim were solidified only as late as the twentieth century. 'Hindu' was defined by the Hindu Code Bill in 1955 as anyone who is *not* Muslim, Christian or Parsi. That is the official definition of Hindu in this country—if you are not this, that or the other, you are Hindu, despite your protestations to the contrary. (The Jains and the Ramakrishna Mission, for example, have gone to court claiming they are not Hindu, while Sikhs demand periodically not to be covered by Hindu laws, all to no avail).

Similarly, the Shariat Act of 1937 fixed the boundaries of the 'Muslim' community, codifying a field of heterogeneous practices among communities that did not all necessarily see themselves as 'Muslim' in the same way.

The Hindu Code Bills, passed in 1955 and 1956, are normally seen as a departure from tradition and orthodoxy, allowing Hindu women, for the first time, to choose their marriage partners, to marry outside their caste, and to divorce, while substantially enhancing a woman's right to her husband's or father's property.

But first of all, who are 'Hindu' women? The assumption that there ever existed a homogeneous Hindu community, is the very first problem. Under the label of 'Hindu', came large numbers of heterogeneous communities living in the land mass called India, with diverse practices—there were communities with matrilineal inheritance practices; there were communities in which women had the rights to divorce, re-marriage and widow marriage; there were innumerable forms of the marriage ceremony. Some feminists argue that one of the goals of the Hindu Code Bills was, in fact, to bring about uniformity among these practices (to codify them) as a national integration measure, rather than to give women any rights (Parasher 1992). The assumption that bringing about uniformity as such is a progressive measure, is deeply problematic. For what the Hindu Code Bills did achieve was the codification of the vast and heterogeneous practices of communities that were not Muslim/Parsi/Christian, bringing them into conformity with what was assumed to be the 'Indian' and 'Hindu' norm—that is, North Indian, upper-caste practices. Other practices that did not match this norm were explicitly dismissed during the debates in Parliament as being un-Indian.

The debates in Parliament over the passing of the Hindu Code Bills reveal the deeply patriarchal and parochial views of the majority of the elected representatives of the Indian people, most of whom were in fact upper-caste and North Indian men (Kishwar 1994; Sinha 2007). Invariably, practices that differed from the upper-caste North Indian norm were either not considered at all or rejected, enshrining only one kind of practice as truly Hindu and Indian.

For instance, here's an exchange in Parliament during the debate on property rights for women, including the devolution, or passing on of a women's property after death:

> Mukut Behari Lal, arguing against property rights for daughters gave, as supporting reason, the fact that no Hindu parent would want to inherit a daughter's property in the event of her death.
>
> To this, L. Krishnaswami Bharathi asked, 'Why not, why not, what's the harm?'
>
> Another MP, called Bhargava, agreeing with Lal, responded, 'Perhaps my honourable friend comes not from India but from some outside country.'
>
> Bharathi: I come from south of India.
>
> Bhargava: In India, no father or mother will ever think of receiving anything from the daughter.
>
> Bharathi: That may be so in the Punjab.
>
> Bhargava: It is so in the whole of northern India, therefore, the entire fabric of the rules of devolution is based on anti-Hindu ideals.

Another instance of such disregard for practices in the south is visible in S.P. Mookerji's comment, speaking against making divorce less complicated: 'Somebody said . . . that south India was specially progressive and many of the laws we are considering are already in existence there today. I say, good luck to south India. Let south India proceed from progress to progress, from divorce to divorce . . . why force it on others who do not want it?' (Kishwar 1994).

Madhu Kishwar also shows that the Hindu Women's Right to Property Act passed under British rule in 1937, that gave Hindu widows rights to their husbands' property, because it applied uniformly to all communities classified as 'Hindu', empowered Brahmin widows, but took away from Jain widows the much better provisions that they had had under customary law. The 'reformed' law thus worked to the detriment of communities that had better inheritance practices for women than Brahmins.

This Act also established *saptapadi* (a Brahminical marriage ceremony) as the norm, thus delegitimating other forms of marriage that were (and continue to be) widely prevalent. The effect has been that, despite the fact that bigamy is outlawed, a second marriage is impossible to prove in court if the bigamous man has followed some other form of customary marriage, thus freeing him from responsibilities to both the women involved (Agnes 1999).

The Hindu Succession Act (HSA) nullified the better position of daughters under matrilineal laws, making sons equal inheritors. Originally, matrilineal communities had been exempted from the purview of the Hindu Code Bill, but the Select Committee headed by Ambedkar, against his judgement, removed the exemption. While empowering men under matriliny, the HSA refused women from non-matrilineal communities (the vast majority), rights to coparcenary property (a situation rectified only as late as 2005). At the same time, the safeguards for women that existed in the traditional coparcenary system were done away with. The main feature of the traditional Hindu joint family property had been its inalienability—that is, it could not be partitioned and sold. But the English concept of alienation through testamentary succession (by writing a will) was incorporated, while the protection granted to family members under English law was not. As a result, the earlier rights of daughters to be maintained from the ancestral property were lost, while their new rights to a share of their fathers' self-earned income, were nullified by the new testatory rights that the fathers simultaneously acquired, to write wills disinheriting them. Interestingly, Flavia Agnes points out that during the parliamentary debate, these very features disempowering daughters were specifically cited as the positive aspects of the new law, in order to persuade members opposing women's property rights, that the new provisions could be circumvented! (Agnes 1999).

When the possibility of equal property rights for women was being discussed in Parliament during the passage of the Hindu Code Bill, M.A. Ayyangar burst out with the terrible image: 'May God save us from having an army of unmarried daughters!' He had got it right of course—the only way to save patriarchal arrangements is by keeping women property-less and dependent on fathers, brothers and husbands. At least he was honest about it, unlike our suave twenty-first century patriarchs.

It seems to me that the personal laws on succession and property, such as the Hindu Succession Act, represent a point of conflict between the imperatives of the State and of those of the family. The modern State requires legibility in order to mobilize resources towards capitalist industrialization, that is, it must be able to 'see' and recognize the forms of property in existence. Towards this end, the institution of individual rights to property is crucial. All forms of property must become completely alienable and transparent to the State—this development is essential for capitalist transformation of the economy. The family, on the other hand, has its own imperatives of controlling name, descent and passing on of property—a project disrupted by individual property rights. In the light of this, we must view the gradual granting of property rights to women under Hindu law as more than a simple triumph of feminist demands—it also represents the establishment of a bourgeois regime of property for the Hindu community at least in principle, which makes land completely alienable by every separate individual owner. In the current climate of widespread resistance to land acquisition, this is a considerable achievement for the State, as it always easier to pressurize or tempt individual owners, rather than communities, to sell land.

It is in this context also that we must understand feminist legal scholar and activist Nandita Haksar's critique of some feminist initiatives to press for individual rights to property of tribal women over community rights. She sees such initiatives as uncomprehending of the complex community practices that make up tribal understanding of property and its ownership. She urges the need for a struggle within tribal communities to evolve new customs that are more egalitarian, rather than forcefully introducing, from above, individual rights to property (Haksar 1999).

The process of rendering uniform a multiplicity of practices among 'Hindu' communities was often justified by the claim that this was a step towards a uniform civil code for all communities. However, among the four acts passed was the Hindu Minority and Guardianship Act (1956), which was a step *away* from the secular laws applying to all communities. It took Hindus out of the purview of the existing Guardians and Wards Act of 1890 that had hitherto applied to all communities. What this new law accomplished was that it established an aspect of 'Hindu Shastras'—'father as natural guardian'—as the law of the land for Hindus while, under the earlier law, court-appointed guardianship would supercede the 'shastric' idea of 'father as natural guardian' (Sinha 2007). Court-appointed guardianship had tended to retain de facto guardians—in most cases, mothers (Kishwar 1994). Thus, this new law both reinforced 'Shastras' for Hindus over secular law, and disempowered Hindu mothers.

Later, another little lollipop for Hindu men—the only secular law on marriage, the Special Marriage Act, was amended to exclude Hindu men from its more gender-just property provisions, and to give them the protection of the Hindu Succession Act. (Hindu right-wing politicians often claim that the 'minorities are appeased'—it seems to me that it is the men of all communities who are routinely appeased.)

The last vestiges of Nair matriliny that had gradually been delegitimized, were finally eroded with the Hindu Succession Act of 1956. Historian Praveena Kodoth has pointed out that this dispossession of women was produced within a narrative of historical progress and the newly-emerging discourse of individual rights. That is, the end of Nair women's exclusive rights to natal property under matriliny was conducted impeccably in the language of rights—pitting the rights of the 'wife' against those of the 'sister' of the Nair man; the subject of rights was never, of course, assumed to be the Nair woman herself (Kodoth 2001).

Here's a story my mother tells from our own matrilineal past: her brother, my maternal uncle, at the age of eight, in the early 1940s, sat studying his English primer, rocking back and forth, muttering loudly, 'Family means wife and children, family means wife and children'. Their grandmother, hearing him, was appalled. She raged up and down the house: 'Is this the kind of Western nonsense they're teaching children in school now? But family means sisters and *their* children . . . no wonder tharavadus are collapsing one by one . . .' Bleakly, she faced a world in which brothers would abandon their families, their sisters, their nieces and nephews; a world in which a woman had nothing unless she was a wife. For her, the tharavadu was the natural institution; it was the patriarchal nuclear family that was a bizarre Western practice.

Over a period of about half a century, these processes nation-wide, enabled the family in its current form to appear natural and unchanging. The three key interlinked features of this 'Indian' family are—patriarchy (power distributed along gender and age hierarchies, but with adult men trumping older women); patriliny (property and name passing from father to son); and virilocality (wife moving to the husband's home.)

In this configuration, patrilineal virilocality is the key, isolating women from all previous support systems and leaving them entirely at the mercy of their husbands' families.

In this context, here's a revealing development—it was recently reported that the Punjab State Commission for Women (PSCW) had issued a brochure in Punjabi advising young women to stop using mobile phones to keep in touch with their natal families if they wanted to keep their marriages intact. Faced with criticism, the chairperson of PSCW clarified: 'I found that almost 40 per cent of women consider seeking a divorce on the grounds that their husbands and in-laws do not like their talking on mobile phones.' Apparently, the husbands and their family members suspect that the women are talking to other men over the phone. Even if the women are only calling their parents, said the chairperson, that's a problem, as being in constant touch with their natal homes hampers their adjustment into their new homes (AFP 2011).

Clearly, mobile phones prevent the crucially necessary isolation of new brides from their natal families!

WHAT'S IN A NAME!

Another feature of this new form of family that has become increasingly ubiquitous, is the phenomenon of the changing of the woman's surname upon marriage. Surnames themselves are relatively new in India, and emerged under

British rule, with the previous practices of naming being gradually reshaped to fit the new State's requirements of legibility. This phenomenon is found in all British colonies, by the way (Scott 1998). Along with the emergence of the surname, one sees the emergence of *Mrs X*, X being the surname of the husband and, sometimes, his first name if he has not adopted the surname format—as many have not yet—in south India, for example. The idea of women not changing their surname upon marriage, is thus, not so much a 'Western feminist' idea, but rather for us in India, could be seen as a return to one's traditions! Every Indian family today has to go back only a generation to remember how different naming practices used to be, and to consider the implications of that for women's identity. The surnames that emerged under colonialism are simply caste names, of course, and thus we see also the move to drop surnames as a deliberate political act, by Dalits as well as by non-Dalits.

Often, in discussions on feminism with young people, I have been challenged by the smart alec (usually male) in the room with the question: If a woman doesn't change her surname on marriage, what's the big deal? After all, her own surname is only her father's name, it's just another man's name. I have found this question striking in its assumption that a man's surname is his 'own', not his father's name; while the woman's surname always remains 'her father's'. After all, I reply, by not changing her surname, a woman is simply choosing her own father's name over her husband's father's name! It is also striking when this question comes, not from traditional patriarchs, but from young men in college, thoroughly modern, having thoroughly internalized Western patriarchal norms as natural.*

Recently, in what could seem like a paradoxical act, feminist lawyer Flavia Agnes successfully fought for the legal right of a divorced woman to continue using her married surname. The passport office had refused to renew her passport in her married name since she was divorced, but all her other documents were in that name, and a change in this one key document would mean immense hardship for her. Many divorced women have suffered because of this approach, said Agnes. Here, the feminist concern is that women should not have to suffer an additional burden after a divorce—that of legally changing their names back to their previous ones. Additional Solicitor General Darius Khambata, in a legal opinion to the Mumbai Regional Passport Office, held that 'The wife has a fundamental right under Article 21 of the Constitution of India (right to life) to use any name, including her married name, notwithstanding the fact that her marriage has been dissolved', provided her husband has no objection (Deshpande 2011). Of course, if a husband objects to a divorced wife using 'his' name, then she has to give it up.[5]

So, divorced women have to give up their husbands' names if the husbands insist, but what about women who had not changed their names upon marriage? There is absolutely no legal requirement that women should take their husbands' surnames but, even in the absence of any such specific regulation, minor officials of the State—passport

---

* Sometimes I feel like saying to them, at least defend your own damn patriarchy!

staff, for instance—often reinforce certain assumed norms of the family. There have thus been many instances of married women who have retained their surnames, being forced by passport authorities to change their surnames to match their husbands', or to add them to their own surname. They are given no choice in the matter (Sharma and Arora 2011).

Thus there are two issues here—the emergence of the universal 'surname' as part of the homogenizing practices of the modern colonial state and the wife taking the husband's name as a natural and unquestionable part of marriage. What we see in the interlinking of the two is the gradual naturalization of two dominant patriarchies—North Indian upper-caste and British colonial.

(PUBLIC) CITIZENSHIP AND (PRIVATE) FAMILY

The gendering of citizenship requires us to question and to challenge the fact that citizenship, a supposedly public identity, is produced and mediated by the supposedly private heterosexual patriarchal family. Feminist thought thus recognizes the patriarchal family as the basis for the secondary status of women in society, and hence the feminist slogan— 'The personal is political.' That is, what is considered to be 'personal' (the bedroom, the kitchen), has to be recognized as completely submerged in power relations, with significant implications for what is called 'the public' (property, paid work, citizenship)—it is, therefore, 'political'.

Take for instance, the Supreme Court judgment (of 2005) which ruled that a child inherits the father's caste. It thus held illegal the election of an upper-caste man's daughter from a constituency reserved for a candidate belonging to a Scheduled Tribe. In her petition defending her election which had been challenged by the defeated candidates, Shobha Hymavati Devi had argued that her father had not legally married her mother (belonging to the Bagatha, a Scheduled Tribe), whom he had abandoned along with his children by her. Therefore, since Shobha Devi was brought up by her mother in her community, she should be considered to have inherited her mother's caste. The Justices of the Supreme Court were not impressed by this reasoning. Indeed, they expressed their 'dismay' that a politician, in her bid for political office, would stoop so low as to 'brand her five siblings and herself illegitimate and her mother, a concubine.'[6]

There are two implicit assumptions at play in this judgment—one, that 'illegitimacy' is something that any respectable person would try to hide, and so a declaration of illegitimacy could only be a ploy to hold on to office. Two, the three upper-caste judges constituting the Bench seem to share the general, upper-caste, anti-affirmative action understanding in India that a Scheduled Caste/Scheduled Tribe (SC/ST) identity is an undeserved advantage that must be limited as far as possible.[7] Thus, while the judgment has the potential to be read subversively as establishing a precedent to recognize women's rights in common law marriage as well as to legitimize inter-caste marriage, its underlying assumptions establish it instead, as a precedent for naturalizing caste identities passed on through patriarchy.

Another instance is a defeated Bill that sought to deny Kashmiri women the right to permanent citizenship of the state of Jammu and Kashmir if they married outside the state.

A J&K minister defended the Bill against the charge of being anti-women with the argument that, since non-Kashmiri women who married Kashmiri men would get citizenship rights in the state, the loss of rights by one set of women would be balanced by the gain of another set. On the whole, therefore, women as such would not lose out. That this argument can make any sense at all has to do with the way in which the rules governing the institution of the heterosexual patriarchal family are assumed to be natural, eternal and part of the human condition. The assumption is that all women get married and get (some) rights as wives, somewhere. By implication, non-married women do not need rights to property. In this sense, the J&K Bill is no anomaly—it simply gives formal recognition to the actually existing secondary status of women and the meaning of marriage in the rest of India.

For another example, take the Madhya Pradesh government's 'Mukhyamantri Kanyadan Yojna', a scheme meant to help girls from poor families get married at government expense.[8] Marriages under the scheme are solemnized free of cost and all arrangements are made by the district administration. Every couple is also provided assistance in the form of household items worth Rs 5,000. Here, the state government takes over the father's role in perpetuating marriage as an inevitable and unavoidable fate for all. After all, this money could have been used to train young women in some skill, or to set them up in a small business. However, this criticism of the scheme has never been made. But in July 2009, the news broke that 'virginity tests' were being conducted on the women, and there was an uproar (Ghatwai 2009). Of course it was obnoxious, but then, isn't it equally obnoxious that every father who gets his daughter married, in effect, also guarantees her virginity? Isn't that what *kanyadan* implies? If the government takes over the father's responsibility of marriage, why is it surprising that it takes over the father's responsibility of ensuring the daughter's chastity? This is what I meant by saying that only in extraordinary circumstances does the violence implicit in the institution of the family become visible; under 'normal' circumstances, it is, precisely, normalized.

As it happens, in this case, the explanation given was that several already-married couples were lining up to get married under this scheme in order to avail of the wedding gift, and the virginity test was intended to weed out such couples; the assumption being that unmarried women would, of course, be virgins! This Kanyadan Yojana is remarkable for exposing the key patriarchal assumption that underlies family and marriage—the need to control women's sexuality—and, by relocating this assumption to the 'public' as opposed to the 'private', revealed it in all its misogyny.

Another revealing instance of how marriage is understood by the State is provided by Section 497 of the Indian Penal Code regarding adultery, under which a man can bring a criminal case against another man for having an affair with his wife. The wife is not culpable under this provision, nor can a woman use this provision against another woman or against her husband. The assumption is that the wife is the husband's property, a passive object over which no other man has rights. Thus, the very assumptions of this provision are sexist and patriarchal and therefore, feminists are appalled by the recommendations of the Law Commission of India and the National Commission for Women that this provision be made gender-neutral to bring women under its purview. As recently as 2011, the Bombay High Court upheld the criminalization of adultery as essential for preserving the sanctity of marriage.

The criminalization of consenting sex between adults is unacceptable. Certainly, adultery by either partner may be treated a 'fault' that can be the basis for a divorce, but it cannot be treated as a criminal offence. This provision has no place in a modern legal code, and must be struck down.

We need to create conditions for marriage to be seen as an option to be chosen freely, with the in-built possibility of a fair divorce, for which an equitable partition of household resources is essential. As long as women do not have equal rights in marital property, the majority of women who continue to be by far the weaker party in any marriage, and who contribute to the husband's income only through non-tangible 'non-work', will be left with no economic security or even a roof over their head after a divorce. The government has drafted a Bill (in 2010) to introduce 'irretrievable breakdown of marriage' as a ground for divorce in the Hindu Marriage Act, and women's groups are concerned that it is being rushed through without ensuring equitable partition of household property and wealth (Singh 2012).

UNDERSTANDING DOWRY

We move now to an issue on which there appears to be little difference of opinion—dowry, denounced as an evil across the board. But what is dowry? Scholars of the practice say that it has changed so much over time, and refers to such a wide range of practices of gift-giving in marriage, that it is difficult to define. But in its most basic form, it can be understood as a form of inheritance of parental property prior to the death of the parents, for daughters who otherwise lack inheritance rights. It is because of this aspect of dowry that some argue against a dowry boycott without strengthening women's inheritance rights, since dowry provides women with at least some form of property that could stand them in good stead in their marital homes. However, others argue that dowry is transacted between the men of the two families, and the control over a woman's dowry lies not with her but with her husband and his family. What has also become visible in South Asia since the 1980s is the violence associated with dowry—its non-voluntary character, oppressiveness and systematic dowry-related violence against women in their marital homes.

Feminist writer C.S. Lakshmi has linked dowry to the compulsory nature of marriage itself, and to the way it alienates women from their natal families. She tells us about a question addressed to the well-known social reformer and anti-dowry activist of the early twentieth century, Sister Subbalakshmi: 'What if women cannot get married because they refuse to give a dowry?' Sister Subbalakshmi's response was, 'Then, women must have the dignity and courage to remain single.'[9]

In this sense, say some feminist scholars, the issues underlying dowry can be related to the condition of women under Western patriarchies as well—that is, gendered subordination built into the political economy of compulsory heterosexual marriage, women's unequal access to financial resources, and the widespread physical and structural violence against women. The point here is that dowry-related violence is not unique, but only a specific South Asian expression of gendered violence that is present in different ways in different parts of the globe (Basu 2009).

Srimati Basu argues that the Dowry Prohibition Act (amended in 1984) is ineffective because it can do little to address the social mechanisms through which dowry flourishes, and it can come into play only if a complaint is filed. It must also be noted that complaints are never about demands for dowry as such, but about 'exorbitant' or continuing demands for dowry after some dowry has already been given. But the fact that both the giver and the taker of dowry are held to be equally culpable by the Act also means that there is an inbuilt disincentive to report demands for dowry, except after death or in association with other lawsuits (Basu 2009:181). Indeed, in 2009, a judgment by a sessions court in Delhi, on a complaint filed by a woman against her husband's family for dowry-related violence, ordered that the woman's father too, should be prosecuted under the Act for having given dowry (Anand 2009). This is why women's organizations working on the issue prefer to use a range of other legal options that address concrete problems within marriage—economic subservience, lack of residential options, and domestic violence—rather than the Dowry Prohibition Act itself. These options include pursuing divorce along with Section 406 of the Indian Penal Code for criminal breach of trust if dowry goods are not returned;

Section 498A relating to cruelty by husband or his relatives; and the Domestic Violence Act (2005) which gives women rights of residence in the marital household.

Dowry was essentially a North Indian Hindu upper-caste practice but has gradually spread to almost all classes, castes, regions and religions in India. The reason for this spread is said by different scholars to be a combination of 'sanskritization' (a sociological term meaning 'emulation of upper castes'); increasing consumerism and marketization; and the rise of cash incomes associated with the liberalization of the economy in the 1990s (Tomalin 2009).

I would like to suggest here that the spread of the practice of non-voluntary dowry and related violence, must be directly linked to the gradual spread of a particular form of marriage and family which, by the late twentieth century, had come to appear natural in India. That is, the emergence of the patriarchal, patrilineal, virilocal marriage as the universal form of marriage, from among all the heterogeneous marriage and property practices that had existed in different communities earlier. The expansion of dowry to every community in India must be seen as the consequence of the emergence of this one form of the family in every community—compulsory marriage that sends women away to husbands' homes to adjust, manage and survive or not, as they will; and that gives women limited rights to property as a wife, never as a daughter. As long as this form of the family is seen to be natural and inevitable, and as long as marriage under this form is compulsory for everyone, attempts to end the 'evil of dowry' are doomed to failure. Dowry, as a problem, cannot be resolved without restructuring the contemporary family form.

THE IMPLOSION OF MARRIAGE?

This form of family is an inherently violent institution that is gendered to the core. I do not refer here to instances of physical violence specifically; I mean that the institution as such, and the form it has come to take all over India, involve a violent reshaping of the self of the woman getting married. We have not considered adequately what patrilineal virilocality does to a woman. She leaves her home, whether parental or living by herself as a professional, and goes to her husband's home or to that of his parents. She changes her surname, in some communities even her first name, and her children bear their father's name; thus, her own name, even if she is one of the rare instances of retaining her name after marriage, is obliterated.

Women have to learn to remake themselves completely, but even more significant is the fact that the entire period of their lives before this singular event of marriage, is spent in anticipating and preparing for this specific future, from choice of career and job options to learning to be adaptable from early girlhood.

As a young girl said, 'Whenever I tell my mother to have fun, go out, wear interesting clothes, she says, "Now I am married, I can't do that." If marriage is the end of life, how can it also be the goal of life?'[10]

This is the background in which we must address the common questions often thrown as a challenge to us: But aren't women women's worst enemies? Isn't the mother-in-law the cruellest to the daughter-in-law? Why is this so? Before we attempt an answer, let us consider a different, rarely-asked question: Why are there no battles for power between the father-in-law and the son-in-law? Because their spheres are entirely different. Because the power game between them is not such that increased power for one means reduced power for the other. But women in virilocal households derive their power solely from men—their husbands, and then their sons who eventually become some other woman's husband. Power struggles between women are inbuilt in this kind of structure, and are inevitable. This is not because they are 'women', but because they are put into positions that are pitted against one another. Imagine a situation in which fathers-in-law and sons-in-law routinely have to face off against each other in a limited sphere assigned to them, in which, gradually, the son-in-law will take over from the father-in-law. Men would be men's worst enemies then.*

Just to go back to that taunt, though, that women are women's worst enemies—when we understand the structure of the patriarchal virilocal family, we can see that it is tailor-made to pit women against each other.

This engrained violence of marriage is what in fact, cannot be addressed, women have no language in which to address this. Hence, I think, the widespread use of Section 498A and allegations of dowry demands, that has come to

---

* When one thinks of the hundreds of bitter property battles between fathers and sons and between brother and brother, one might want to say that men are already men's worst enemies!

be called 'misuse' of these provisions. Since dowry involves the property of the natal family, the woman can expect or at least, hope, to get their support by citing dowry; indeed, part of the arbitration by women's groups is often directed to getting back the dowry. Police and lawyers too, on getting complaints of domestic violence, often encourage the invocation of the Dowry Prohibition Act, as a quick and easily recognizable remedy.

The 'misuse' argument made by men is, in this sense, ironically correct in terms of how patriarchy is supposed to work. These men actually believe they are 'falsely accused' because what they are saying in effect is: 'This is what a family is supposed to be; as a wife, you are supposed to give up everything that you thought you were; we have expectations of you, which you are supposed to fulfil. This is marriage'. And women are refusing to recognize this as marriage. Men are right to say, in this sense, that they are being 'falsely' accused—because all they were doing was functioning as a proper patriarchal family.

There is no explanation available for the woman's unhappiness at her changed state. Can a woman just go back home saying simply: '*I don't want to be a wife, I don't like this job?*' Forcibly trained from girlhood for marriage and marriage alone, not permitted to dream of any other future, expecting that marriage will be the beginning of their lives, and finding that it is in fact the end of their lives; the frustration and resentment that this situation generates has led increasingly to what I see as the *implosion of marriage*—young girls simply refusing to perform the role of the docile wife and daughter-in-law, to the bewilderment and rage of the families into which they marry. These legal provisions essentially treat the family as a public institution to which public laws apply. Obviously, this creates a crisis for the family, leading to the idea that it is men who need to be protected from 'draconian' laws around marriage. But the overwhelming majority that suffers is still women, most of whom invest so much energy, so much courage, so much strength, in simply staying on in violent, humiliating marriages.

However, a thoroughgoing critique is essential, not just of the marital family, but of the natal/parental family. Even after one daughter is married off and killed for dowry, her parents' idea of a secure future for their second daughter, too, is marriage. A parallel phenomenon is the violent 'ragging' in professional training institutions—young boys facing physical and emotional torture from senior students are repeatedly told by their parents to go back to their institutions, to bear it, to think of the expenses involved, to think of their future careers, to bear it and bear it until, finally, they are killed. The family's job is, after all, to produce men and women who will not rock the boat, who will fulfil their parents' expectations—of social status, of insurance in old age. For instance, Ravinder Kaur's work on agricultural families in Punjab has shown that not even all sons are equally desired, bachelor sons are considered to be expendable (Kaur 2008). The patriarchal family as such—whether the conjugal (post-marriage) or the natal (into which the woman is born)—is a site of violent power play and exclusions.

There are growing indications of the implosion of this form of marriage and family. A newspaper story in late 2011 reported that in Haryana, a state with a marked degree of son-preference and one of the lowest sex ratios in India, about 'half-a-dozen notices appear daily in vernacular and English newspapers' from fathers, sometimes mothers, publicly disowning sons and daughters, and debarring them from their property (Siwach 2011). Although such notices have no legal sanction, they reveal the explosive tensions that are just barely contained within the framework of the family.

NEW REPRODUCTIVE TECHNOLOGIES A CHALLENGE TO PATRILINY?

New technological developments in reproductive science have made it possible to separate three different aspects in the biological experience of motherhood. Three different women could potentially perform what I term the key 'mother functions'—providing genetic material (the egg donor); gestating the foetus for nine months (the surrogate or 'gestational mother'); and rearing and bringing up the child (the 'social mother'). In the older biological understanding of motherhood, these three functions are assumed to be fused in one woman; but now there could be two or three women performing these three separate roles in each pregnancy.

Thus, a woman can now carry in her uterus through in vitro fertilization (IVF), that is, fertilized outside the body, an embryo that could be from her own egg or another woman's, fertilized by a donor's sperm or that of her husband or lover. The child born out of this process is often meant for someone else to bring up (surrogacy), but women may also opt for their own child using this process. This means that a woman who does not want a man in her life can become pregnant through donor sperm; this process may also be used by married women if they or their husbands cannot produce the required quality of egg or sperm.

There are legitimate feminist concerns about the exploitation of poor women who perform commercial surrogacy, which we will address in a later section. But what are the implications of these technologies for a feminist understanding of 'family'? Here, the most significant feminist concern is that the promotion of these technologies by major drug companies and market forces, reinforces the patriarchal assumption that only biologically related children are one's 'own', thus attempting to marginalize the option of adoption. At the same time, though, many feminists also recognize the potential of these scientific-technological developments to fracture, in principle, patriarchal constructions of 'motherhood' which conflate the social role with 'biology'. That is, what does it do to the idea of 'motherhood' once the 'womb' (the surrogate) has been separated from the 'mother' (the 'social' mother who will bring up the child)? And is it not possible that these developments could potentially reduce the heterosexual monopoly over the family by enabling 'socially infertile people' as Chayanika Shah terms them—that is, single women, single men and same-sex couples—to have biologically related offspring?

It is also important to open up and unravel the very idea of 'biologically' related families, which are assumed to be the only kind of family possible. In the context of new reproductive technologies, we find that potential parents contracting with a surrogate are reassured by drug companies and medical practitioners that if the genetic matter is theirs (that is, the egg and the sperm), then the child is 'biologically' theirs, since the surrogate's womb only acts as 'an oven', 'a rented room', and so on. However, in cases in which a woman wants to carry a donor sperm and a donor egg IVF baby for herself, in her own womb, then the same companies and doctors reassure her that the real work of 'making the baby' happens in the womb, and the baby is, in fact, 'biologically' related to the woman in whose womb the foetus grows.[11]

In other words, as we have seen already, 'biological' relationships are also socially constructed. Like most technological developments, then, the social implications of surrogacy would vary from context to context.

*

The family is an institution that rigidly enforces systems of inheritance and descent and in this structure, individuals— sons, daughters, wives, husbands—are resources that are strictly bound by the violence, implicit and explicit, of this frame. We tend to take this frame for granted, and it becomes obscenely visible only in extraordinary circumstances.

As feminists, we need to build up the capacity and the strength of both women and men to live in ways in which marriage is voluntary, and to build alternate non-marriage-based communities.

If the marriage-based family is the foundation of the social order as it exists, at the heart of that family is an identity that we now need to destabilize—sex difference.

BODY

'If they see breasts and long hair coming,
they call it woman.
If beard and whiskers they call it man.
But look, the self that hovers in between
Is neither man nor woman . . .'

THE BODY IN EARLY MODERNITY AND
IN NON-WESTERN CULTURES

The first thing to note is that the rigid division of bodies into 'male only' and 'female only' occurred at a particular moment in human history, that is, at the inception of the constellation of features that we term 'modernity'. Thus, a set of assumptions that form common sense today were absent in Europe prior to the late sixteenth century, and in South Asia and Africa until the early nineteenth century, when European modernity was universalized through colonialism. That is, assumptions such as the idea that nature exists separately from humans as a passive, inert set of resources to be put to human use; that bodies are naturally entirely one sex or another; that hermaphroditism (bodies possessing both male and female sexual characteristics) is a disease; and that desire naturally flows only between 'opposite' sexes. Anne Fausto-Sterling points out that in Europe, it was only by the seventeenth century that hermaphrodites were forced to choose one established gender and stay with it, the punishment being death for failing to do so (2002).

The key notion central to European modernity which enables the 'common sense' assumptions outlined above, was the putting in place of the notion of the individual— that 'I' am this body and that 'my self' stops at the boundaries of my skin. Although this seems an entirely natural identification to the modern mind, it is in fact only about four hundred years old and has specific cultural moorings in the experience of the West. In non-Western societies this notion of the individual, separate from all other individuals, as the unit of society, is still not an uncontested one. At every level in non-Western societies then, there remains a sense of self that is produced at the *intersection* of individuated bodies and collectivities of different sorts. Individuation then—that is, the process of recognizing oneself as primarily an individual—is always an on-going process *in the present continuous* in our parts of the world.

It is against this backdrop that we must ask the question: Was sex/gender a *universally* relevant criterion of social differentiation at all? That is, did all societies at all times and in all places make male/female distinctions that sustained themselves over stable bodies?

This question is raised frontally by Nigerian scholar Oyeronke Oyewumi, who challenges the universality of gender as a social category. She argues that Western anthropologists, even feminists, failed to understand African society in its own terms, because they assumed that gender identities and hierarchies were universal: 'If the investigator assumes gender, then gender categories will be found whether they exist or not.'

Oyewumi argues that the emergence of patriarchy in the West as a form of social organization is rooted in particular assumptions that emerged with modernity in the West— the gradual privileging of gender difference as the primary difference in society, and locating this difference in certain visual cues. (The blue-for-boys-pink-for-girls principle as it emerged in the West is an instance of this, and we will return to its surprising history a little later).

Oyewumi makes the radical suggestion that 'gender' as a category did not operate in any significant way in pre-colonial Yoruba and many other African cultures. For instance, she cites a study of the Ga people in Accra (Ghana) by a Western anthropologist, who began by looking for 'women', tracked those 'women' in the processes of their work, and found they were overwhelmingly traders. The author of that study conceded, 'I started out to work with women; I ended by working with traders.' Oyewumi asks the question: 'Why did the author look for "women" in the first place? Her answer is: 'because "woman" is a body-based identity, and body-based identities tend to be privileged by Western researchers over non-body-based identities, such as "trader".' The identity of trader in West African societies is non-gender-specific, says Oyewumi, but the Ga traders continue to be referred to in the study as 'market women', 'as if the explanation for their involvement in this occupation is to be found in their breasts, or . . . in the X chromosome.'

Oyewumi argues through her own work that among the Yoruba, *seniority* is the defining axis of hierarchy, not *gender*. Seniority is based not only on chronological birth order, but on interrelationships established through marriage. Thus, seniority is always relative and context-dependent, depending on who is present in any given situation. The Yoruba language is gender-free; Yoruba names are not gender-specific, nor are *oko* and *aya*, usually (wrongly) translated into English as husband and wife; and the terms for 'ruler' too are gender-free (though translated into English as 'king'). Thus, gender is not the relevant category to understand power relations among the pre-colonial Yoruba (Oyewumi 1997).

Ifi Amadiume's work on the Igbo of Nigeria, too, establishes that, in pre-colonial Igbo society, daughters could assume male roles and become sons, and wealthy women could obtain 'wives'. The linguistic system of the Igbo had few gender distinctions, and terms for roles such as 'head of household' were un-gendered, while the 'master' or 'husband' role did not necessitate a male classification. Amadiume terms this 'gender flexibility'. However, we can go further with the framework that Oyewumi provides us, for it enables us to radically interrogate whether the category of 'gender' existed in any recognizable way in pre-colonial Igbo society. Oyewumi insists that the African ways of understanding the world were radically different from the Western, but have been continually translated, even by African scholars, into Western categories and languages already loaded with gendered and patriarchal assumptions. Was 'gender', then, invented in Africa through the processes by which colonial interventions made African societies legible to Europe in its own terms (Amadiume 1987)?

Similarly, in Native American culture, before the Europeans came to the Americas, 'two-spirit' referred to people who were considered gifted because they carried two spirits, male and female. It is told in ancient artefacts that women engaged in tribal warfare and married other women, and there were men who married other men. These individuals were looked upon as a third and a fourth gender, and in almost all cultures they were honoured and revered. Two-spirit people were often the visionaries, the healers, the medicine people, the nannies of orphans, the care-givers. This type of identity has been documented in over 155 tribes across Native North America (Roscoe 1988).

Consider now the poets of the Bhakti movement in the landmass we now call India—this movement originated in the southern part, in the Tamil region in the sixth century CE and flourished in the north from the fifteenth to the seventeenth centuries. These mystics expressed a kind of desire for God that travels through the body and reconfigures it. Their desire was to attain the loss of maleness as power and the loss of femaleness as sexualized powerlessness. A.K. Ramanujan suggests that 'the lines between male and female are continuously crossed and recrossed' in the lives of the Bhakti saints. They demystified the body and sexuality by dismantling the codes and conventions that 'sex' the body. Bhakti saints turned away from sex in this world—not from fear or hatred of sexuality, but because their sexual passion was invested entirely and in a disembodied manner, in the chosen deity as lover.

A tenth-century devotee of Shiva, Devara Dasimayya, wrote:

> If they see breasts and long hair coming,
> They call it woman,
> If beard and whiskers
> They call it man.
> But look, the self that hovers in between
> Is neither man nor woman . . .[1]

Ramanujan points out that when women saints like Lalla Ded of Kashmir and Mahadeviyakka of Karnataka threw away their clothes, they were making us see that 'modesty'—which is invested in hiding the body with clothes—is 'a way of resisting and enhancing sexual curiosity, not of curbing it. It is this paradox that is exposed when clothes are thrown away. By exposing the difference between male and female, by becoming indifferent to that difference, [they are] liberated from it.'

This is how the female saint Mahadeviyakka, who clothed herself only in her own long hair, perceives the body:

> You can confiscate
> Money in hand;
> Can you confiscate
> the body's glory?
> Or peel away every strip
> you wear,
> but can you peel
> the Nothing, the Nakedness
> that covers and veils?[2]

Clearly even by the time of the Bhakti movement, normative notions of masculinity/femininity and appropriate/inappropriate sex had come into being, against which the Bhakti saints were in rebellion. But considerable fluidity still existed even till the mid- to late-nineteenth century, when the processes of colonial modernity, in alliance with the modernizing nationalist élite began the process of disciplining it.

Historical work on cross-dressing (male actors playing female roles) in theatre and dance in late-nineteenth/early-twentieth-century India, at a moment when the practice was beginning to be delegitimized by the discourses of modernity, shows that arguments about gender verisimilitude—that cross-dressing men didn't look feminine enough—were made in order to end the practice of men playing women's roles. But, simultaneously, such arguments displayed an anxiety that female impersonators were so feminine that they could 'soil the fancy' of men! (Bhattacharya 2003). Feminist scholars have shown that female impersonation, far from appearing unnatural, in fact fashioned 'a widely circulated standard for female appearance and modified codes of feminine conduct' (Hansen 1999). Female viewers, indeed, were instructed to model themselves on the transvestite actor. The new nationalist bourgeois woman was to learn how to be a proper woman by watching the production of appropriate femininity by a male actor.

Bindu Menon brings to our attention work about a legendary female impersonator on the Malayalam stage, Ochira Velukkutty. A recent book on a history of women in Malayalam theatre reveals that when Mavelikkara Ponnamma, one of the first female actors on the Malayalam stage, was approached to enact the role of the beautiful Vasavadutta in the play *Karuna*, a role performed and immortalized by Velukkutty, Ponnamma was hesitant since she felt she could never reach the perfection of Velukkutty's performance. Only when she received a letter from Velukkutty (by then ill and bed-ridden), encouraging her to perform the role, did she feel she had his blessings. After this, she says, 'Even my voice changed. I became Velukkutty, and then Vasavadutta'.

Says Menon, 'Having a woman's body was not sufficient to perform women on stage. Femininity was a highly coded practice, and these codes were developed by Velukkutty and similar female impersonators.'[3] This scholarship is but a tiny part of a vast field of work that tracks the ways in which the fluid identities and practices of pre-colonial societies were rendered legible to and by colonial modernity throughout the nineteenth century in India. The process was never 'completed' though, and heterogeneous forms of sexuality continue to simmer below the skin of 'normal' society in the non-West, as we will see.

We should remember that processes of modernity in Europe had already performed this exercise of fixing sexual identity, over the sixteenth–nineteenth centuries. In the twentieth century then, in Europe/the US, there arose significant philosophical and sociological interventions, feminist and non-feminist, that began to question the key concepts that had stabilized as 'natural' by that time—the body, sex, sexuality.

'SEX IS TO NATURE AS GENDER IS TO CULTURE'

The making of a distinction between sex and gender is intrinsic to feminism. The initial move was to use the term 'sex' to refer to the biological differences between men and women, while 'gender' indicated the vast range of cultural meanings attached to that basic difference. This distinction is important for feminism to make because the subordination of women has been fundamentally justified on the grounds of the biological differences between men and women. This kind of philosophical reasoning which legitimizes various forms of subordination as natural and inescapable, because it is based on supposedly natural and, therefore, unchangeable factors—is called biological determinism. Racism is a good example of biological determinism, as is the caste system, because both ideologies are based on the assumption that certain groups of people are superior by birth, and that they are born with characteristics, such as greater intelligence and special skills, that justify their power in society. Biological determinism has also been one of the most important legitimizing mechanisms of women's oppression over the centuries. The challenge to biological determinism is, therefore, crucial for feminist politics.

Feminist anthropologists, pre-eminent among whom is Margaret Mead, have demonstrated that what is understood as masculinity and femininity varies across cultures. Not only do different societies identify a certain set of characteristics as feminine and another set as masculine, but also, these characteristics are not the same across different cultures. Thus, feminists have argued that there is no necessary cor-relation between the biology of men and women and the qualities that are thought to be masculine and feminine. Rather, it is child-rearing practices which try to establish and perpetuate certain differences between the sexes. That is, from childhood, boys and girls are trained in appropriate, gender-specific forms of behaviour, play, dress and so on. This training is continuous and most of the time, subtle, but when necessary, can involve punishments to bring about conformity. So feminists argue that sex-specific qualities (for example, bravery and confidence as 'masculine', and sensitivity and shyness as 'feminine') and the value that society attributes to them, are produced by a range of institutions and beliefs that socialize boys and girls differently. As Simone de Beauvoir put it, 'One is not born, but rather becomes a woman'.

In addition, societies generally value 'masculine' characteristics more highly than 'feminine' ones and at the same time, ensure that men and women who do not conform to these characteristics are continuously disciplined into the appropriate behaviour. For instance, a man who expresses sorrow publicly by crying would be humiliated by the taunt, '*Auraton jaise ro rahe ho*?' (Why are you crying like a woman?) And who does not remember that stirring line of Subhadra Kumari Chauhan's—'*Khoob ladi mardani, woh to Jhansi wali rani thi.*' (Bravely she fought, the Rani of Jhansi/ Like a man she did fight). What does this line mean? Even when it is a woman who has shown bravery, it still cannot be understood as a 'feminine' quality. Bravery is seen as a masculine virtue no matter how many women may display it or how few men.

But of course, what is considered to be masculine or feminine shifts from time to time. Until the middle of the twentieth century in the West, for instance, pink was the colour for boys and blue for girls! In the 1800s, most infants were dressed in white, and gender differences weren't highlighted until well after they were able to walk. At that point of time in the West, it was considered to be more important to distinguish children from adults than boys from girls. But when the interest in differentiating between boys and girls emerged in the early twentieth century, the colour associated with boys was pink, and it was blue for girls. In 1927, *Time* magazine wrote about the disappointment in Belgium at the birth of a girl to the royal family, saying her cradle had been 'optimistically decorated in pink, the colour for boys'. Close to the end of World War I, *Ladies' Home Journal* advised new mothers that 'the generally accepted rule is pink for the boys, and blue for the girls. The reason is that pink, being a more decided and stronger colour, is more suitable for the boy, while blue, which is more delicate and dainty, is prettier for the girl'. Some argued that pink was a close relative of red, which was seen as a fiery, manly colour. Others traced the association of blue with girls to the frequent depiction of the Virgin Mary in blue. It is only in the mid-twentieth century that the opposite colour-coding began to appear 'natural' (Adams 2008; Belkin 2009).

Consider also Fatima Mernissi's work comparing the writings of eleventh-century Islamic scholar Imam Ghazali on sexuality with the writings of Freud. Ghazali, writing in Persia in the eleventh century, believed he was attempting to reveal the true Muslim belief on the subject; Freud, at the triumphant inception of modernity in Europe, could claim the authority of science to elaborate not just a theory about European sexuality, but a universal explanation of the human female. Mernissi shows that while both Ghazali and Freud see female sexuality as destructive to the social order, Ghazali argues this through an understanding of the *active* nature of female sexuality, while Freud makes his argument through an understanding of female sexuality as *passive*.

Mernissi argues that in comparing Freud's and Ghazali's theories, we are, in fact, comparing the different conceptions of sexuality of the two cultures, the former assuming female sexuality to be passive, the latter to be active, but with each seeing women as destructive to the social order, for those entirely opposite reasons (Mernissi 1987).

The initial sex/gender distinction made by feminists, as laid out above, has been complicated in several ways. Many scholars argue that 'sex' and 'gender' are dialectically and inseparably related, and that the conceptual distinction which earlier feminists established between the two is not sustainable beyond a point. In this understanding, human biology itself is constituted by a complex interaction between the human body, the physical environment and the state of development of technology and society. Thus, the hand is as much the *product* of labour as the *tool* of labour—human intervention changes the external environment and, simultaneously, the human body is shaped by changes in the external environment.

This is true in two senses. One, in a long-term evolutionary sense, over the millennia. Human bodies have evolved differently in different parts of the globe, due to differences in diet, climate and the nature of the work performed. Two, in a more short-term sense, in one lifetime. It is now recognized that neurophysiology and hormonal balances are affected by social factors, like anxiety, physical labour, and the level and the kind of social interaction, just as much as social interaction is affected by people's neurophysiology and hormonal balances. For instance, certain chemical changes in the body may produce certain symptoms of stress that can be treated by drugs. But equally, high stress levels can, in fact, be the reason for higher chemical imbalances, and it may be possible to restore the body's balance only by changing the conditions in which it lives (Jaggar 1983).

When we apply this understanding—to the sex/gender distinction—that biology and culture are interrelated—we see that women's bodies have been shaped by social restrictions and by norms of beauty. That is, the 'body' has been formed as much by 'culture' as by 'nature'. For instance, the rapid improvements in women's athletic records over the past two decades is an indication that social norms have shaped the capacities of their bodies. Feminist anthropologists have pointed out that in some ethnic groups there is little physical differentiation between men and women. In short, we must consider that there are two equally powerful factors at work: one, there is a range of interrelated ways in which society produces sex differences; and, two, sex differences structure society in particular ways.

'Sex', seen thus, is not an unchanging base upon which society constructs 'gender' meanings, but rather, sex itself has been affected by various factors external to it—there is no clear and unchanging line separating nature and culture.

A second kind of rethinking of sex/gender has come from a kind of feminism which argues that feminists must not underplay the biological difference between the sexes, and attribute all difference to 'culture' alone. To do so is to accept male civilization's devaluing of the female reproductive role. This is a criticism of the liberal feminist understanding that, in an ideal world, men and women would be more or less alike. The contrary claim is that patriarchal social values have denigrated feminine qualities and that it is the task of feminism to recover feminine qualities as being valuable. Here, the understanding is that there are certain differences between men and women which arise from their different biological reproductive roles and that therefore, women are more sensitive, instinctive and closer to nature. Such feminists are often called 'radical feminists'; they believe that women's reproductive biology—the process of gestation and the experience of mothering—fundamentally affects their relationship to the external world. Women are, therefore, in this understanding, closer to nature and share in nature's qualities of fecundity, nurturing and instinct. These qualities have been rejected by a masculinist patriarchal society but feminists should accept and revalue these qualities.

Eco-feminism, for instance, is a feminist philosophy that celebrates the feminine difference derided by patriarchy. This philosophy points to the predominance of what it calls a masculinist ideology that structures the world, through which both nature and women are to be controlled and dominated, and their productive capacities harnessed for certain kinds of economic goals. Vandana Shiva, for example, shows that both women and nature are thought to be passive by masculinist ideology, productive only if their energies are harnessed in a certain way. A forest is thought of as unproductive unless it is planted with, for example, commercial woods. Unless it is planted with teak and other trees that can be cut and sold, unless something commercial happens, a forest is not thought of as productive. The very term 'natural resource' suggests that nature is merely a resource for capitalism to yield profit, and so, unless the forest does that, it is thought of as non-productive. But Shiva points out that its productivity is actually continuous—a forest is preserving groundwater just by standing there. It's replacing oxygen in the atmosphere, it is providing a habitat for animal species, it is providing food and fuel for local inhabitants. So what eco-feminism tries to do, is reclaim from masculinist ideology a radicalized notion of the creative feminine (Shiva 1988).

Carol Gilligan's book, *In a Different Voice* (1982), uses a psychoanalytical framework to argue that because the primary care-giver in childhood is invariably a woman (the mother)— given the sexual division of labour—the process by which men and women come to adulthood is different. Boys come into adulthood learning to *differentiate* themselves from the mother, while girls do so by *identifying* with the mother. That is, in a sex-differentiated society, while all infants identify with the mother, boys gradually learn that they are 'different' from, while girls learn that they are the 'same' as, their mother. This results, Gilligan argues, in women having a more subjective, relational way of engaging with the world, while men have a more objective, autonomous mode. Women relate to others, while men learn to separate themselves.

Gilligan's focus in this work is the difference in the ways men and women take moral decisions, and she comes to the conclusion that women are less influenced by abstract normative notions of what is right and wrong, and more by contextual factors, like empathy, concern and sensitivity to another's predicament. Men, on the other hand, tend to take moral decisions based on well-accepted, context-free notions of right and wrong. For instance, it is always wrong to steal, no matter what the circumstances. Thus, Gilligan concludes that the basic categories of Western moral philosophy—rationality, autonomy and justice—are drawn from and reflect the male experience of the world. The female experience is invisible here, and women's tendency not to take hard, de-contextualized moral positions is seen by mainstream Western philosophy as a sign of their moral immaturity. To deny difference is, therefore, to agree with the patriarchal negation of femininity as worthless.

Later developments on Carol Gilligan's work showed that the autonomous individual, abstracted from all socio-cultural context, taking context-free moral decisions, is not produced only by 'masculinity', but also by cultural contexts inflected by race. That is, it was found that both men and women of non-white and immigrant communities tended to relate their moral decisions to context, and to be more located within communities than wealthy white men and women. This has resonance with Radhika Chopra's work on South Asian masculinities which she terms 'supportive', as opposed to that of the autonomous disconnected masculinity familiar from Western literature. The patriarchal privilege of South Asian men is defined within a network of responsibilities they are expected to fulfil towards their sisters, younger brothers and parents. Thus, their control and power over women and younger men is mediated by a sense of responsibility towards them that can often be prioritized over their own individual desires and ambitions. Chopra has also pointed out that the institution of domestic servants in South Asia compromises the 'masculinity' of the male domestic servant within an Indian household, vis-à-vis his female employer (Chopra 2003).

Feminism has long recognized that gender identity is not in all contexts the determinant and that other identities—race, class, caste, religious community—intersect and are relevant for understanding particular issues. This will become increasingly clear as we go along.

Now, the arguments discussed above, theorizing cultural constructions around the biological body, all stop at the limits set by the biological body, assuming it to be a given natural object. What has increasingly come into view is a kind of understanding of gender that problematizes the body itself. The body, here, is not a simple physical object but is constructed by and takes its meaning from its positioning within specific social, cultural and economic practices.

'GENDER PERFORMATIVITY'

A feminist philosopher whose name inevitably arises in this context is Judith Butler, whose first book, *Gender Trouble* (1990), is seen as a landmark. Butler argued that if we take seriously Simone de Beauvoir's dictum that one is not born, but *becomes* a woman, it means that all of us have to *learn* to be men and women. If so, there is no reason why 'feminine' qualities should attach only to bodies marked female, and 'masculine' qualities to bodies marked male. She thus suggested a 'radical discontinuity' between sexed bodies and culturally constructed genders.

Butler uses the term *heterosexual matrix* to refer to a sort of grid produced by institutions, practices and discourses—

from biomedical sciences to religion and culture—looking through which, it appears to be 'a fact of nature' that all human bodies possess one of two fixed sexual identities, with each experiencing sexual desire only for the 'opposite sex'. The removal of this heterosexual matrix will reveal that sexuality and human bodies and desires are fluid and have no necessary fixed sexual identity or orientation.

Thus, her startling argument is that 'gender' is not the cultural inscription of meaning on a pre-given 'sex'. Rather, gender as a way of thinking and as a concept, pre-exists the body; it is gender that produces the category of biological sex. And gender produces sex through a series of performances.

We must not understand this 'performativity' as something superficial (that is, mere 'performance' as opposed to 'reality'). Butler's argument is that bodies are 'forcibly materialized over time' by the reiterative, repeated practices of gender performance (Butler 1993). That is, over time, bodies come to meet with the criteria of legibility laid down by the heterosexual matrix—intersex bodies are surgically disciplined into one of two sexes; breasts will be reduced or enlarged, and inappropriate breasts kept hidden and invisible; depilation, clothing and make-up will take care of the rest. We will address some of these phenomena in the next section.

Butler draws attention to the fact that the project of becoming male or female is never completed—it is a 'performance' that must be repeated every moment of our lives until we die. Even a fifty-year-old, burly moustachioed man who has fathered children cannot say, 'It is well established by now that I am a man; tomorrow, I can wear a sari to work.' At no point in our lives can we be confident that our gender identity is secure; we can never let up on this performance.

WHAT ABOUT 'REAL' BODIES?

What is rendered invisible by the 'heterosexual matrix' is the multiplicity of bodies. A range of bodies becomes invisible or illegitimate through the functioning of hegemonic legal and cultural codes. When an idea is 'hegemonic', it has become common sense, and has been internalized even by those oppressed by it.

Since the hegemonic understanding of the human body now is that each and every body is clearly and unambiguously male or female, large numbers of bodies that do not fit this description are designated as diseased or disordered in some way. For instance, infants born with no clear determining sexual characteristics; eunuchs; men and women who have characteristics that are 'non-masculine' or 'non-feminine', respectively. All these have to be disciplined into normalcy through medical and surgical intervention, or they must be declared abnormal or illegal. Our very language, held implacably as it is in the grip of a bipolarity of gender, falters when attempting to refer to such bodies. Is an intersex child he or she, *avan* or *aval, woh karega ya karegi*?

Take, for instance, a revealing letter to the medical column of a newspaper in India, from 'a grieving mother', who seeks advice about her eighteen-year-old son whose sudden depression she traced to the fact that 'his nipples and breasts are bulging out, which disgusts him.' The doctor's reassuring reply is that nearly thirty per cent of men have 'suffered' from what is termed 'gynaecomastia' at some time or the other. In some cases, the cause could be tumours or malnutrition, but this is rare. The most common cause of gynaecomastia, says this doctor, is simply 'pubertal', due to the fact that breast tissue, normally dormant in boys, is 'super sensitive to the minuscule amount of circulating female hormones.' The doctor says that once the 'rare causes' have been ruled out by an endocrinologist, either the condition is self-limiting, or, if it is not, may require surgery.[4]

Nearly a third of the male population can have 'breasts', and if it is not due to rare endocrinological causes, the condition is perfectly normal. It seems to have no other ill effects than causing 'disgust' but, nevertheless, it is pathologized and made into a disease (gynaecomastia), and when other serious illnesses have been ruled out, the advice given is not to relax and stop worrying, but to undertake surgery, to make that body conform to a mythical norm.

In a fascinating study of the emergence of hormones as the definitive marker of gender difference, Nelly Oudshoorn demonstrates that in Western thought—from the ancient Greeks until the late eighteenth century—male and female bodies were understood to be fundamentally similar. This 'one-sex' model of humanity, with the woman as a lesser version of the male body, had been dominant since antiquity. In the eighteenth century, biomedical discourse began to emphasize differences rather than similarities between the sexes, and from the twentieth century, the hormonal conception of the body has become one of the dominant modes of thinking about the root of sex differences. As Oudshoorn points out, the hormonal conception of the body, in fact, allows for the possibility of breaking out of the tyranny of the binary sex-difference model. That is, if bodies can have both female and male hormones, then maleness and femaleness are not restricted to one kind of body alone. However, biomedical sciences prefer to treat the presence of androgen in female bodies and estrogen in male bodies as abnormal. Further, the female, but not the male, is portrayed as a body completely at the mercy of hormones. In this process, a clear nexus has emerged between the medical profession and a huge, multi-billion-dollar pharmaceutical industry. All sorts of 'disorders' in women—such as the aging of the skin, depression, menstrual irregularities—are prescribed hormonal therapy (Oudshoorn 1994). This pathologization clearly extends to male bodies that react to the 'minuscule amounts' (as the doctor in the letter above firmly qualifies), of female hormones circulating in them.

LACTATING MALES, UNMATERNAL FEMALES

I learnt recently that lactation can be induced in adoptive mothers even if they have undergone complete hysterectomies, because prolactin and oxytocin, the hormones that govern lactation, are not produced by the ovaries, but by the pituitary gland. Through a process of preparation involving a hormone regimen and stimulation of the breasts, almost all women can lactate although, despite following protocol, some women may fail to do so. It occurred to me that if pregnancy is not the only condition in which women can lactate, and if the hormones required for lactation are produced by a gland present in all humans then, perhaps, lactation can be induced in men?

Turns out the answer is yes. There have even been recorded instances of men spontaneously lactating; but in any case, through the process described above, it is possible to induce lactation in men if they have babies they want to nurse (Swaminathan 2007; Shanley 2007). Certainly, the breasts will enlarge, and certainly, you will be the freakish guy who lactates. The problem is not that this isn't natural, because really, what's natural about inducing lactation in women?

Male lactation? I bless every little boy out there who thinks that when he grows up, his baby will drink milk from his boo-boos.* May he no longer have to grow up to the devastating recognition of its impossibility!

So, males can lactate, but unmaternal females?

The legendary dancer Chandralekha was once asked a question in a public interview in New York, about whether she regretted not having had children. She is reported to have answered by flamboyantly outlining her breasts in the classical Bharatanatyam style, and declaring, 'My dear, we worship the Goddess as *apeethakuchaambal*—She whose breasts have never suckled.'[5]

Through the figure of female deities powerful in folk and urban cultures, from the dim past of pre-history till this day, Chandralekha (1992) has insisted on the disruption of the fertility/maternality dyad. For her, the fecundity principle

---

* And you all know such boys.

is a mysterious force, over time domesticated into the figure of the 'mother' goddess. She demands,

> On what basis do you call them *mothers*, these dynamic figures of fierce power who look so calm and confident on the bull, the lion, the tiger; who wear weapons as ornaments in their hair, who are not at all maternal?

The 'domestication' of the fierce, uncontrollable fertility associated with nature into tender, vulnerable motherhood is a feature in the historical development of not only Hinduism, but also Christianity.[6]

The unsettling question then is, what happens to our ideas of men and women if we can think of fertility, 'maternal' urges, motherhood and even lactation, as separate features of the human condition, regardless of the gender that is assigned to the body?

'IF MEN COULD MENSTRUATE'

Menstruation is certainly one feature inescapably associated with the female body. But the ways in which it acts as a disability have to do with social and cultural, not natural constraints. American feminist Gloria Steinem wrote a savagely funny meditation on what would happen to the understanding of menstruation in a patriarchal society, if men could menstruate. Since everything that men do is valued, the fact that men could and women could not menstruate would become yet another indicator of the superiority of men:

What would happen, for instance, if suddenly, magically, men could menstruate and women could not?

The answer is clear—menstruation would become an enviable, boast-worthy, masculine event:

Men would brag about how long and how much.

Boys would mark the onset of menses, that longed-for proof of manhood, with religious ritual and stag parties . . .

Sanitary supplies would be federally funded and free . . .

Military men, right-wing politicians, and religious fundamentalists would cite menstruation ('men-struation') as proof that only men could serve in the Army ('you have to give blood to take blood'), occupy political office ('can women be aggressive without that steadfast cycle governed by the planet Mars?'), be priest and ministers ('how could a woman know what it is to give her blood for our sins?') or rabbis ('without the monthly loss of impurities, women remain unclean').

She imagines headlines like 'Judge cites monthly stress in pardoning rapist' (Steinem 1978).

The fact remains that something which affects half the population is simply absent in the public consciousness. Clean and plentiful public toilets and inexpensive and easily accessible sanitary napkins would make monthly periods for most women simply routine. But because the public realm is structured around the assumption of the able male body (and in India, one that can use any public space to urinate or defecate), this seriously compromises normal (let alone efficient) functioning for women outside the home.

The Indian market in sanitary napkins is controlled by two multinational companies, Procter & Gamble and Johnson & Johnson. The overwhelming majority of women in India make do with extremely cumbersome and inescapably unhygienic ways of dealing with their periods. State subsidy for sanitary napkins should be routine, because they are unaffordable for most women, and given that the Indian state still does subsidize commodities, from diesel to condoms. But recently, Indian feminists encountered a strange situation.

In 2010, newspapers reported government plans to supply free sanitary napkins to an estimated 200 million rural women, at a cost to the government of Rs 2000 crores annually. What is disturbing is that it seemed that this project would be in collaboration with one of the two MNCs, which would then be the chief financial beneficiary. Around the same time, it emerged that a social entrepreneur had developed a low-cost sanitary napkin-manufacturing machine within the financial reach of rural women's self-help groups, who were availing of bank loans to buy it. This project was already being implemented in about 200 places across India and, in Maharashtra, the state government is associated with it. Banks would be even more willing to give loans to self-help groups for purchasing the machine if the government would guarantee that it would buy back the napkins from them. This would not be more expensive than the other project, which would benefit only the MNCs. This alternative would also be sustainable and generate employment while making women's lives easier (Kumar 2010). At the time of going to press, nothing further was known about the government decision.

The point is that the 'disability' of any natural bodily function can and must be understood as a product of its inescapable *social* dimensions.

INTERSEX

Intersex people are born with both ovarian and testicular tissue or with ambiguous sex organs. Intersex people, hermaphrodites, as they used to be called, were not a problem for society until the rigid male/female binary was constructed with the coming of modernity. In the West, from the twentieth century, it became common for doctors to assign one sex or the other to intersex babies, and to make surgical interventions to match this assignment. A study conducted of intersex babies and sex assignment in the US showed that medical decisions to assign one sex or the other were made on *cultural* assumptions rather than on any existing *biological* features. That is, in some cases, the parents 'wanted a girl/boy' (with all the cultural expectations that 'being a girl/boy' involves). In some, the tissue available could be fashioned either into a satisfactory clitoris or a small penis and, given the general assumption that to live as a man with a small penis is to be avoided at all costs, the decision would be to make the child into a girl. And so on. Thus, a baby might be made into a female or a male but then would still require hormonal therapy all her life to make him/her stay in the surgically assigned gender (Kessler 1990).

Recently, a sensationalist and irresponsible piece of reporting in an Indian national daily claimed that in the city of Indore, hundreds of female babies were being surgically turned into boys to fulfil the preference of their parents for sons. There was immediate and widespread outrage from feminist groups as well as government agencies until finally, an investigative report in another newspaper clarified the situation (Jebaraj 2011). The report quoted doctors as stating that it is medically impossible to change a female child into a male, and that what had been carried out in Indore was a legitimate medical procedure called 'genitoplasty' for male infants 'born with abnormal genitalia.' This procedure is described in the newspaper article as 'a corrective surgery for babies, regularly recommended by paediatricians and urologists for a child with congenital abnormality of the genitalia. For example, the penis may be small or seem missing because it is buried under the skin due to abnormal curvature.'

'It is about making a male child a better male, functionally or structurally. It's not about converting a child's sex,' said a doctor.

It is still not clear whether these babies were born intersex, but the report also cites a study by India's premier medical institution, All India Institute of Medical Sciences, which found that 'in cases of extreme ambiguity, where the child is considered "intersex," the doctor must "assign" the sex of the child before deciding how the genitalia are corrected'. The AIIMS study admits that 'The gender assignment takes into account the prevalent social factors in a community and the parents' desire.' This is not unusual as we saw earlier in the case of the US-based study. This could well mean, said the report, that in some cases, the desire of Indian parents for a boy could influence the doctor's assignment of sexual identity. The writer also pointed out that there is a wider international debate on whether corrective surgeries should be done at all on such children, or whether 'intersex' children should be left to decide their own sexual identity upon reaching adulthood.

There is, of course, another possibility—that they could live perfectly healthy and fulfilling lives as intersex people, even being capable of reproduction. So the only reason to shape them into the either/or pattern is cultural, not 'biological'. There is a growing intersex movement globally, that draws attention to the fact that treating the intersex condition as a disease is a phenomenon that started in the nineteenth century in the West. The goal of intersex advocacy groups is to have people understand the intersex condition, not as a disease, but as a perfectly 'normal' way of being. As the website of Intersex Society of North America puts it:

> Intersex is a socially constructed category that reflects real biological variation . . .
>
> . . . Nature presents us with sex anatomy spectrums. Breasts, penises, clitorises, scrotums, labia, gonads—all of these vary in size and shape and morphology. So-called 'sex' chromosomes can vary quite a bit, too. But in human cultures, sex categories get simplified into male, female, and sometimes intersex, in order to simplify social interactions, express what we know and feel, and maintain order.
>
> So nature doesn't decide where the category of 'male' ends and the category of 'intersex' begins, or where the category of 'intersex' ends and the category of 'female' begins. Humans decide.

In India, queer groups are in touch with a few people who acknowledge their intersex condition but publicly live as either male or female. There has generally been no conversation that they have had with their parents or their doctors about their condition. Thus, they live in the sort of loneliness experienced by many others who have to hide important parts of their identities.[7]

The question then really, is this:

WOULD YOU PASS A GENDER TEST?

'Gender verification' tests for the Olympic Games were suspended in 2000 after enough evidence had emerged that 'atypical chromosomal variations' are not atypical at all, but rather, so common that it is impossible to judge 'femininity' and 'masculinity' on the basis of chromosomal pattern alone. Maleness and femaleness are not only culturally different, they are not even biologically stable features at all times.

But in sports, as in all other spheres of life, despite evidence to the contrary, it continues to be assumed that every human being can be assigned to one of two sex categories. Thus, the Olympic Committee retained a policy of 'suspicion based testing' on a case-by-case basis, as did other sports bodies. This policy at different times resulted in two women athletes—South African Caster Semenya and Indian Santhi Soundarajan—being disqualified after winning their events, for failing 'gender tests'. Their experiences raise a host of questions about this biological body that is considered to be simply available in nature.

Three sets of characteristics are held to determine sexual identity:

a) genetic—the XX female and XY male chromosomal pattern;
b) hormonal—estrogen (female), androgen/testosterone (male); and
c) genital—the visible physical characteristics of penis/ vagina.

However, feminist scholars of science studies have directed our attention to developments in biology that show that the three are not necessarily linked. Thus, if a body has female genitals it is not necessarily the case that it would have preponderantly female chromosomes and female hormones. Moreover, sex chromosomes themselves often defy the pattern of XX (women) and XY (men) and have been known to exhibit other patterns, such as X0 (females with only one X chromosome), XXY, XYY, XXX, or a 'mosaic condition', in which different cells in the same individual's body have different sex chromosomes (Buzuvis 2010).

Most bodies (including yours and mine) marked male and female in this world would not pass 'gender tests' if the perfect congruence of these three factors were being examined. The point is that in everyday life, gender tests are not routine because once a sex has been assigned at birth, one lives one's life accordingly.

It is mainly in sex-segregated activities like competitive sports that the question arises, and only for women, because it is assumed that having male characteristics is an advantage in physical activities. Thus, 'real' women would face the unfair advantages that 'not women' have on the field. Of course, women athletes who are disqualified for some chromosomal, hormonal or physical variation that casts doubt on their 'femaleness', do not get categorized as 'men'. They are still excluded from men's sports events and professions reserved for men.

At least two questions arise here. First, how fair are competitive events that assume male bodies to be the norm, so that to have male features is an advantage? This only reflects the general understanding that any quality associated with men is superior and must set the norm for all humanity. In whichever ways women are different, their difference is considered to be an *inferior* difference, not *just* a difference, or a *superior* difference.

But the second more fundamental question here arises from the fact that not all natural advantages are considered illegitimate in sports. For instance, height in basketball is an accepted natural advantage, while American Olympian swimmer Michael Phelps's particular body proportions that enable him to cut through water more easily than 'normal' men may, in fact, be a disease called Marfan Syndrome.[8] Different ethnic groups have different physical characteristics, such as height and build. The point is, really, that competitive sport does not sort out competitors on the basis of comparable physical features and athletic ability—there is no level playing field. Men of different physical attributes, levels of training and differential natural advantages such as height and strength, compete against one another, as do women. Is it not important to ask why the only standard of difference applied is that of an assumed gender bipolarity? To put it in the striking words of one scholar:

Saying that no one can use natural advantage is antithetical to sport. The average individual does not become a world-class or Olympic athlete . . . [Those who excel in sport have genetically acquired physiological advantages whose potential has been realized fortuitously through cultural and environmental factors]. Yet, for conditions other than those related to sex, such variation is not challenged as beyond the bounds of fair play (Buzuvis 2010).

Consider an intriguing story from the war zone of the sports field. In the 1936 Olympics, Polish sprinter Stella Walsh, known as the fastest woman in the world, was beaten by American Helen Stephens, who set a world record. After the race, a Polish journalist protested that no real woman could run so fast, and Olympic officials performed a 'sex test' on Helen, in which it was established that she was a woman. Forty-four years later, Stella Walsh, who had become an American citizen, was shot to death in a parking lot. The autopsy of her body revealed that Stella, who had run slower than Helen, had in fact 'been a man' (Boylan 2008). Another strange story from the same Berlin Olympics—twenty years afterwards, a Hitler Youth member who had competed as a woman and ranked fourth in the women's high jump event, confessed he was a man who had been forced by the Nazis to compete as a woman. This 'real man' came fourth, behind three women (Buzuvis 2010).

All men do not run faster than all women; all men are not stronger than all women; all men do not jump higher than all women; and this is why it has often been suggested by feminists that athletes should be categorized on the basis of physical characteristics relevant to the sport, rather than on the basis of sex.

The point is that we are not clearly-bounded male and female bodies with immediately obvious male and female characteristics, with only a few abnormal people not fitting the bill. When a child is born, it is usually the presence or absence of a penis that dictates gender assignment. But children who don't have penises do sometimes have internal male reproductive organs and XY chromosomes. Because females are defined in terms of *lack of penis* rather than *presence of vagina and uterus/ovaries*, it is quite common for children who are genetically male to be raised as female.

Even more fascinating is the discovery of recent biological research that hormones to some extent are produced by gendered activity rather than the other way around. Aggressive interludes produce increased androgen, while periods of non-aggression—nurturing of infants or of the elderly and so on—produce a reduction in androgen. Thus, feminist scholars of science reject the idea that scientific facts about the body simply exist to be discovered. Rather, scientific facts are deeply embedded in society and culture. 'Sex' itself is constructed by human practices, of which 'science' is one.

Historian of science, Emily Martin, draws our attention to the fact that science, far from simply describing natural phenomena, is in fact an interpretive exercise. She shows us that science tells the story of the process of human reproduction in such a way that the Egg and the Sperm are cast into roles drawn from narratives of heterosexual romance in the contemporary Western world. We are all familiar both with such romance narratives (active energetic hero, passively waiting heroine) and the narratives of biology textbooks (active sperm, passive egg). In biology textbooks, the egg is 'passively transported', is 'swept', or 'drifts' along the fallopian tube, waiting for the active sperm to take the initiative and make her fulfil her *raison d'être*. Once released from the ovary, says a standard textbook, the egg will die 'unless rescued by a sperm'. 'It is remarkable,' says Martin, 'how "femininely" the egg behaves and how "masculinely" the sperm.'

New research has suggested that the sperm's motion is not strong enough to propel it forward, and that, in fact, the egg's surface exudes an energy that actively draws the sperm towards itself, where it is held fast by the adhesive surface of the egg. Martin points out that even these revelations did not lead to a more interactive view of their relationship. Instead, either the 'aggressive sperm' metaphor continued to be deployed, or another cultural stereotype came into play, that of woman as an aggressive and dangerous threat to male autonomy. Martin suggests that an alternative model is already available in the field of biological sciences that can be applied to the egg and the sperm—the cybernetic model with its conception of 'feedback loops' and 'flexible adaptation to change'. Such a model would enable a reading of the egg and the sperm as interacting on more mutual terms (Martin 1991).

In this context, let us consider a literary recreation of the journey of the sperm towards the egg by an early modern feminist writer in Malayalam, Lalitambika Antarjanam. In a short story (1960), she envisages the egg as the female deity, towards which thousands of anxious sperms yearningly travel as pilgrims, a journey in which only one will find self-fulfilment. The narrative is in the exalted, trembling voice of one sperm.[9]

This account, too, draws on local cultural resources—in this case, Mother-goddess worship in Kerala—and is explicitly a creative exercise, reworking the roles that modern science attributes to egg and sperm. Here, the womb is the sanctum sanctorum of the deity; the egg, maternal feminine energy with magnetic power; while for (Western) science it's a Mills & Boon romance!

Evidently, modern scientists, as much as the creative writer, equally use emotive and locally relevant cultural metaphors to describe a supposedly objective 'natural' process.

MALE BODIES AND MASCULINITIES

Masculinity has been theorized for a while now in different ways. In *The Intimate Enemy*, Ashis Nandy made the argument that pre-modern Indian society was marked by fluid gender identities, a fluidity erased by masculinist British imperial ideology. His reading of Gandhi as a figure embodying sexual ambiguity—his political style incorporating key elements of the feminine—has become very influential (Nandy 1983).

Sudhir Kakar, a practising psychoanalyst, argues that the hegemonic narrative of Hindu culture, as far as male development is concerned, 'is neither that of Freud's Oedipus nor of Christianity's Adam. One of the more dominant narratives of this culture is that of Devi, the great goddess, especially in the inner world of the Hindu son.' However, unlike Nandy, he does not see this as a sign of fullness and completion, or of fluidity, but as a fantasy that produces particular forms of misogyny. The most salient feature of male fantasy in India, he argues, is the composite figure of the sexual mother (who inspires rage) and the unfaithful mother (who inspires dread). This mother 'pervades Gandhi's agonizings but also looms large in clinical case histories, myths and in popular narratives'. While across patriarchies a common response is to view women as dangerous antagonists to be subdued, Kakar says the 'defensive mode' of Indian male fantasy takes a specific form—that of 'desexualization, either of the self or of the woman', the former through celibacy and ascetic longings, and the latter through transforming the woman into either a maternal automaton or an 'androgynous virgin'. On the basis of his experiences as a psychoanalyst, Kakar suggests that a sublimated form of femininity in masculine identity may be more acceptable in India than in some other cultures, including the greater acceptability of bisexuality amongst men (Kakar 1989).

An interesting reading of feminized masculinity in Hindu culture is offered by Anuradha Kapur's study (1993) of the transformation of Ram from Tulsidas's gentle, boyish, androgynous body, whose feet were wounded by the grass in the forest and who cried bitterly at Sita's abduction, to the hypermasculinized, aggressive Ram of the Hindu right-wing Ramjanmabhoomi movement of the twentieth century that led to the demolition of the Babri Masjid.

Deviant male bodies too, face disciplining procedures and marginalization—the gay male body, the effeminate male body, the aged male body. Visibly 'effeminate' men often face ridicule and even physical violence on the streets, while aged male bodies (that are not powerful through wealth or social status) are marginalized, often humiliated by younger men and even women. Male domestic servants in the South Asian context embody a 'subordinate masculinity' that renders them 'not-male' vis-à-vis the men of the house, since they perform the tasks allotted to women. With regard to their female employers, their masculinity is often rendered irrelevant, but can also be perceived as dangerous and threatening, making them even more vulnerable to disciplining for perceived crossing of 'limits' (Chopra 2006).

Thus, masculinity too, is produced differently at different intersections of age, class, race, caste, and so on.

It seems that the last bastion of sex difference, the body itself, is revealed to be, not simply given by nature, but made visible in specific ways by different kinds of discourses. Of course, we do experience the world and live in it, in embodied ways. If the body we inhabit is marked male, it has one kind of effect; if female, another kind of effect; if Black, or Dalit, or disabled, yet other effects. These effects are simultaneously structural, material and psychological. But the point is that the body by itself does not produce effects—these are produced by its location in a world structured around certain qualities, assumed to be universal. For instance, the world assumes sightedness and the ability to walk to be the norm; but in a world structured around sightlessness and wheelchairs, it is the sighted person and the person walking on two legs who would have to struggle to manage—steeped in darkness; hearing-impaired, touch-impaired; slipping down steep ramps ...

As we live out these identities, we either reaffirm their worth and value, or reject them and actively seek others. What does this mean for feminism? Is it liberating to realize that the body is not our prison, that it has long histories of being understood and experienced in multiple ways? I think the answer is yes.

DESIRE

'What links queer people to couples who love across caste and community lines is the fact that both are exercising their right to love at enormous personal risk.'

SECTION 377 OF THE INDIAN PENAL CODE

When a lesbian couple has to seek court intervention to stop police persecution initiated by parents, as happened in Kerala a few years ago; every 'lesbian suicide' in which a woman kills herself, leaving behind a letter to say she loves a woman but is being forced into a heterosexual marriage; every story about a physical attack on a gay man—every single one of these incidents starkly underlines the fearsome question that lurks unrecognized at the heart of Section 377 of the Indian Penal Code: Is it natural to be normal?

Section 377 penalizes sexual activity 'against the order of nature'. The assumption is that 'normal' sexual behaviour springs from nature, and that it has nothing to do with culture or history or human choices. But what if we consider the uncomfortable idea that the rules regulating sexuality are produced by different human societies in their different contexts, and don't just spring from nature?

Think about this—if 'normal' behaviour were so natural, it would not require such a vast network of controls to keep in place. Rigidly-gendered dress codes, for example. Imagine a bearded man in a skirt in a public place: why would this shake the very foundations of 'normal' society? Unless 'he' is recognizably a *hijra*, and that would put him on the margins of normal society in a different way. Just the wrong kind of clothes on the wrong body, and the very foundations of natural, normal, sexual identity start to quake? How natural or normal are they, then?

The disciplining of thought through families, the media, education, religion—all telling you that desire for someone of the same sex is a sin, or insane, or criminal. But if it comes unbidden to you, this desire, and it has to be frightened out of you, then which is 'natural'—the thought or its disciplining?

If all else fails, then violent measures are taken to keep people heterosexual—from electric shock therapy to physical abuse to using the coercive apparatus of the State, as the parents in the Kerala incident did. Why would we need laws to maintain something that is natural? Are there laws forcing people to eat or sleep? But we need a law to force people to have sex in a particular way?

But of course, the really interesting thing to consider is that human beings do not, in fact, live particularly 'natural' lives. The whole purpose of civilization seems to be to move as far away from nature as possible. We clothe our naked bodies.* We cook raw food to transform it from its natural state, we build elaborate shelters from the natural elements. We use contraception.**

Clearly, selectively equating 'unnatural' with 'immoral' is simply a way of suffocating debate. It seems then, that Section 377 does not refer to some unnatural people out there, on

---

* Indeed, the same people who condemn homosexuality as unnatural would raise a furore about public nudity.

** Again, most of those who condemn homosexuality on the grounds that sex should only be for procreation, would not question the need for contraception. Only the Pope is consistent in this regard!

whom normal people can gaze like anthropologists at a bizarre tribe. Section 377 is about the painful creation of Mr and Mrs Normal—it is one of the nails holding in place the elaborate fiction that 'normality' springs from nature. Its continued existence is crucial for protecting systems of descent and property. Consider that 'sodomy' or anal sex would be seen as a crime under this Section even in a heterosexual relationship, even within marriage, and consensually.

COLONIAL MODERNITY AND THE PRODUCTION OF HETERONORMATIVITY

The term 'heteronormativity' refers to the overwhelming power of the assumption that heterosexuality is natural and normal, and is the norm to be emulated. It is important to remember that the criminalization of same-sex activity is no ancient Indian tradition, but a legal provision introduced as late as the nineteenth century by the British colonial government. This provision was introduced into the criminal statutes of all British colonies at around the same time. Ruth Vanita and Saleem Kidwai (2000) point out that Britain's own anti-sodomy law was an improvement, in the sense that it reduced the punishment for sodomy from execution to ten years of imprisonment. But its introduction in India in 1861 as Section 377 of the Indian Penal Code introduced a criminalization of practices hitherto invisible to the law. Its wording is general enough to allow any sexual act to be interpreted as coming under its ambit, for it prohibits 'voluntary carnal intercourse against the order of nature, with any man, woman or animal'.

There is abundant scholarship which establishes that the delegitimation of homosexual desire and the production of the naturally heterosexual, properly bi-gendered (unambiguously male *or* female) population of citizens, with the women respectably desexualized, is a process that is central to nation formation all over the globe.[1] A significant instance is the fascinating account of Iran's 'long nineteenth century' by Afsaneh Najmabadi who argues that it was the cultural encounter with Europe that produced in Iran 'the heteronormalization of love and the feminization of beauty'. That is, in Persian aesthetic traditions prior to the European encounter, it was the male body and the love of men for men that was considered beautiful. Thus, says Najmabadi (2005), the modernist project of women's emancipation in Iran bore the 'birthmark of disavowal of male homosexuality'. Women's emancipation was tied to Victorian notions of proper sexual relationships which, of course, delegitimized everything but the heterosexual, patriarchal, monogamous family unit.

In India too, there was a polyvalence of gender identities and sexual desire even up to the nineteenth century, which was closed off in a variety of ways, through legal and social interventions that disciplined a range of non-normative sexualities and family arrangements. Ruth Vanita and Saleem Kidwai in their path-breaking collection, *Same-Sex Love in India*, trace from about 1500 BC up to the present, writings in Indian languages about love between women and love between men who are not biologically related. It is only in the nineteenth century, Vanita and Kidwai argue that 'a minor homophobic voice that was largely ignored by mainstream society in pre-colonial India . . . becomes a dominant voice'.

'QUEER' POLITICS . . .

Is there a 'gay gene'? Rather than argue that there is nothing natural about heterosexuality, should we establish that homosexuality too, is natural? Some prefer this strategy: if homosexuality is genetic, then nobody who is homosexual can help it, God made them this way. It also makes homosexuality seem less threatening: it cannot convert or proselytize, or spread like a disease—you are either born homosexual or you are not.

This is where we come to the politics of naming and language. Many political groupings have come to prefer the term 'queer' to 'LGBTI' (Lesbian, Gay, Bi-sexual, Transgender, Intersex). The latter term can freeze identity, because, to the original LGBT, Intersex has been added on as a separate identity, and so was h for *hijra*, k for *kothi*, and so on. Every new initial fixes as an 'identity' a form of sexual desire or behaviour. 'Transgender' generally refers to men and women who undergo hormonal and surgical interventions to become a person of a sex 'opposite' to the one into which they were born; but is also used as a self-description by many who choose to live their lives in a gender opposite to the one they were assigned. *Hijras* are also transgender in a sense, but this term refers specifically to a traditional community of men who have undergone castration—referred to as *nirvana*—or at least, aspire to that state. *Hijra* now includes within its ambit men who live their lives as women within the community, with or without castration. Intersex, as we saw earlier, refers to a condition in which one's sexual organs are ambiguous.

The point is that once we give up on the idea that only heterosexuality is normal and that all human bodies are clearly either male or female, more and more kinds of bodies and desires will come into view. Perhaps also, one body may, in one lifetime, move through many identities and desires. The use of 'queer' then, is a deliberate political move, which underscores the fluidity (potential and actual) of sexual identity and sexual desire. The term suggests that all kinds of sexual desire and identifications are possible, and all these have socio-cultural and historical co-ordinates. In fact, Anne Fausto-Sterling argues on the basis of the range of bodies that exist in nature, that there are at least five sexes (2002).

In India, from the 1990s, there came to be visible a range of political assertions that implicitly or explicitly challenged heteronormativity and the institution of monogamous patriarchal marriage. Such challenges—we could term them 'counter-heteronormative'—are seen around the demand for the repeal of Section 377 of the Indian Penal Code, and various kinds of political action around issues related to the lives and civil liberties of *hijras,* gay, lesbian, bisexual and transgendered people and sex workers. Of course, counter-heteronormative identities and communities of different sorts have a much longer history in India, as Vanita and Kidwai show, but it was in the 1990s that they came to be visible in public.

Why the 1990s? From the late 1980s, the growing awareness about the AIDS epidemic made it increasingly legitimate to talk of sex outside the realms of law, demography and medicine. It became possible to talk about sex not only as violence against women or in terms of 'population control'. Although AIDS is a disease which also fits into medical discourse, the source of AIDS made sex itself speakable. For example, a highly political, left-wing, non-funded group supporting the rights of homosexuals, which filed a petition against Section 377 in 1992, called itself AIDS Bhedbhav Virodhi Andolan—Movement against AIDS-based Discrimination—'AIDS', in effect, acting as a code for homosexuality. Sex workers' unions, such as Durbar Mahila Samanwaya Committee in Kolkata, and Sampada Grameen Mahila Parishad (SANGRAM) in Sangli (Maharashtra), both started as peer-education programmes distributing condoms as part of an HIV-control project. They now function like trade unions, protecting their members in various ways, organizing street demonstrations, initiating legal action against police violence, and standing up to local criminals.

International funding for HIV/AIDS prevention played a significant role in the creation of new NGOs dealing with sexuality, or funded sexuality programmes in old ones. Once such programmes were started—telephone helplines and safe spaces, for example—it opened the floodgates for political articulation of non-normative sexualities. Autonomous women's groups had, since the late 1970s, been discussing sexuality, including lesbian sexuality and had forged links with international women's groups. But awareness of AIDS finally helped produce a critical mass of such an understanding in the public realm in India. It provided the opening and the monetary resources for public articulation of issues around sexuality; for workshops and meetings which provided often startling new perspectives; brought together people from all over the country with international participants; and mobilized such politics at a countrywide level.

The flip side of this is that official discourse of HIV/AIDS control and the funding generated by it is extremely State-centric, and is about new ways of regulating and controlling sexuality and the population as a whole. However, its effects are uncontrollable, and spill over into forms of radicalization the State could not have predicted nor desired. Nevertheless, the presence of large numbers of NGOs receiving funding for AIDS-related work makes it necessary to maintain a distinction between political practice that is self-consciously counter-hegemonic, and the increasingly acceptable discourse about homosexuality that is restricted to AIDS-prevention.

But the whole unpredictable thing about politics is that often, counter-hegemonic voices are able to tip the scales within a constellation produced by a heterogeneous range of ideas and circumstances. Thus by 1998, when Deepa Mehta's film *Fire* depicting a sexual affair between sisters-in-law in a traditional Hindu household was attacked violently by the Hindu Right, there was a sufficiently self-aware community for the attack to act as a catalyst for public demonstrations in defence of freedom of expression and against homophobia, on the streets of Mumbai and Delhi and some other cities, of a size and visibility unknown before in India. These demonstrations brought together opponents of the Hindu Right, defenders of freedom of expression, human rights activists, and gay and lesbian activists—of course, many or all these categories overlapped.

Another factor that made sexuality visible in public spaces, both élite and non-élite, was the opening up of the media in the 1990s, as part of structural adjustments in the Indian economy. Sexually explicit and suggestive images from the West flowed into homes through private cable television channels, rendering ordinary a large range of images and behaviour that had hitherto been considered unspeakably salacious.

It is significant that counter-heteronormative movements in India should have turned to the women's movement as a natural ally. In the 1980s, the initial response of the established leadership of the women's movement was entirely homophobic, denouncing homosexuality as unnatural, a Western aberration and an élitist preoccupation. Even today, the alliance is not without its problems, but there have been significant shifts. An important landmark is the 1991 National Conference of Autonomous Women's Movements in Tirupati at which an open and often acrimonious discussion on lesbianism took place, with the greatest hostility coming from leftist groups, decrying lesbianism as an élitist deviation from real political issues. Since that time, there has been intense dialogue within the women's movements, and great shifts in perception have taken place, especially on the Left. Openly homophobic arguments are almost never made (publicly) any more within the women's movement.

But there continues to be the sort of argument which suggests that sexuality is less urgent than the bigger issues facing the women's movement. Arguments about priority and élitism have historically been made by left movements to counter feminism, and it would be a pity for feminism to do the same to queer politics. But today, it is clear that challenges to heteronormativity are an unshakeable part of the agenda of feminist politics in India, however contested it may be internally.

From the beginning the term queer in India has gone beyond sexuality. The editors of a volume subtitled, *Queer Politics in India*, hold that:

> The term queer ... speaks ... of communities that name themselves (as gay or lesbian for example), as well as those that do not, recognizing the spaces for same-sex desire and sexuality that cannot be captured in identities alone ...
>
> Queer politics does not speak of the issues of these communities as 'minority issues' but, instead, speaks of larger understandings of gender and sexuality in our society that affect all of us, regardless of our sexual orientation. It speaks of sexuality as politics, intrinsically and inevitably connected with the politics of class, gender, caste, religion and so on, thereby both acknowledging other movements and demanding inclusion within them' (Narrain and Bhan 2005: 3-4)

Voices Against 377, a broad coalition formed to campaign for the abolition of Section 377, links same-sex desire to women's rights, child rights, anti-communalism and anti-war politics.[2] PRISM, a 'non-funded, non-registered feminist forum of individuals inclusive of all gender and sexual expressions and identities' seeks to 'link sexuality with the other axes of construction and control, such as gender, caste and religion' while simultaneously demanding of progressive movements that they should 'engage with issues of marginalized sexualities as an intrinsic part of their mandate' (Sharma and Nath 2005: 82–3).

This knitting together of sexuality with wider left-wing politics can paradoxically, also be limiting for a queer politics of sexuality. Alok Gupta reflects on the reluctance of gay men in Mumbai to make a broader political commitment to the 'larger queer community', which includes, in his account, '*hijras, kothis,* lesbians and women's activists' (and, of course, many gay men). He points out that while Gay Bombay parties can attract up to four hundred men, barely a handful show up for political action. The reason for this reluctance could be caution about public political participation and sometimes, inter-organizational rivalry, but one of the significant reasons, Gupta suggests, is Left influence on the queer movement, which is 'not a bad thing by itself, but it ends up excluding a lot of others.' As a young gay man said to Gupta—'Just because I am gay and identify as queer, and am interested in supporting the movement, I don't want to have the same commitment for people being displaced by unruly dams or bashing America . . .' (Gupta 2005: 138–9). Clearly, just as with feminism itself, queer politics can have many, often mutually-contested, strands.

The other factor Gupta draws to our attention is the operation of class within queer politics. He defines class for the purposes of his analysis, in terms of access to money and the ability to speak English. People who identify themselves as *hijra* or *kothi* (who have been very visible in public queer political action) are not, in this sense, of the same class as the urban élite likely to identify themselves as gay/lesbian/transgender/queer. It is significant, he points out, that while upper-class and middle-class activists of the queer movement to whom he spoke did not think of class as a problem, 'almost everyone I spoke to from lower-class backgrounds felt class to be one of the major barriers facing the community at large.' In a society of strong and visible class differences, this is not surprising, and the temporary resolution that has apparently been worked out, he says in an insightful and troubling recognition, is to draw a line between social and political spaces; that is, to party and mingle informally only with 'people like us', while accommodating more socially diverse groupings on political platforms.

. . . AND FEMINISM

Queer politics and counter-heteronormative trends complicate notions of women and gender. They also complicate the answer to the questions: Who is the subject of feminist politics? Can gay men be the subject of feminist politics? How about transpeople—both male-to-female and female-to-male?

Consider the following troubling example. Some *hijras* claim the right to be recognized as 'women', and a prominent banner at the World Social Forum, Mumbai (2004) said, *Hijras are Women*. Since *hijras* speak of themselves as neither men nor women—although they use the feminine gender in referring to themselves—this banner requires some explanation. It came out of a context in which, in 2002, two High Court judgments set aside the election of two *hijras* from posts reserved for women. The banner was a protest against these judgments. People's Union for Civil Rights, Karnataka (PUCL–K), an organization that brought out a powerful report on human rights violations of *hijras* in Bengaluru, criticized the judgments on the grounds that they 'essentially imply that one cannot choose one's sex and that one should remain within the sex into which one is born' (PUCL–K 2003: 51).

The questions that arise here, however, are more complicated than that. The judgments were not reflecting on identity but on the even more fraught question of political representation of identities. Who can make the claim to represent a particular identity—this is the question here. *Hijras* continue to hold elected posts in general (un-reserved) seats, and these judgments did not affect them. The identity of *hijras* is not in question here. Nor is the fact that *hijras* today are among the most marginalized of communities in India, often reduced to the borders of criminal extortion (in the guise of demanding traditional gifts at weddings and childbirths) in order to make a living. They are routinely harassed by police and physically threatened and/or assaulted under the umbrella of Section 377. Their specific needs for a dignified existence are not addressed by any political grouping, and certainly not by the women's movement. Many *hijras* are also sex-workers, and it is as sex workers that they have become politicized, and in sex workers' unions that they find some of their demands articulated. The PUCL–K report, in fact, is a study of transgender sex workers in Bengaluru.

However, the question is—can *hijras* represent women in constituencies reserved for women? It is, after all, not the biological category of 'woman' that requires reservation, but particular kinds of materially located experiences that need to find space in representative institutions. The point, therefore, is not whether one can biologically become a woman at any point in one's life, but whether the *experiences* of women of different classes and castes can somehow be written into parliamentary discourses. Thus, if we are to think of ways in which the experiences of *hijras*, among other identities, are to be similarly written in, then we must think of more radical alternatives than simply divide up representation between 'men' and 'others'. The experience of oppression that *hijras* have, is not reducible to the experience of 'women'. Therefore, I find more promising another strategy followed by *hijras*—the demand to be recognized as a third gender. A few years ago, as the result of long-term lobbying by NGOs working on sexuality and human rights, a provision was introduced whereby, on Indian passport forms, *hijras* could write 'E' in the column which requires M/F for 'sex'.[3] The recognition of several genders and of multiple and shifting ways of being constituted as political entities may be able to help generate new ways of thinking about representative institutions in a democracy. We will return later to the complicated question of reservations for women in representative institutions.

The possibility of alliances between *hijras*/transpeople and the women's movement faces questions not immediately amenable to any clear resolution. Urvashi Butalia raises some of these questions in the moving account of her friendship with Mona, a *hijra* in Delhi. Mona was born male but from the moment she became conscious of herself as a person, she was convinced she was born into the wrong body. 'I really wanted to be a girl', she told Butalia. Suffering throughout her childhood for her 'girlishness', she came into contact with *hijras* at the age of eighteen, and that changed her life forever. She went with them to get castrated, a procedure known in the *hijra* community as *nirvana*, after which she felt an 'enormous sense of liberation'.

Butalia, the feminist, with all the feminist discomfort about notions of some essential 'femaleness', wonders what it was about 'femaleness' that so attracted Mona. Then, when Butalia's father passed away, Mona visited her mother and consoling her, said that she knew what it was like to be alone, without a man. This too, Butalia found paradoxical, coming from someone who had spent her life rejecting her masculinity. And yet, never fully rejecting it because as Butalia found, Mona drew on her 'maleness' whenever she needed clout, a resource that Butalia herself could never have (2011).

Are *hijras* then, part of the 'women's movement'? Not a question amenable to an easy resolution, and we will have to keep talking and thinking, and arguing. In the meanwhile, listen to the powerful and moving voice of a hijira, A. Revathi, telling her own story in *The Truth About Me* (2010).

DELHI HIGH COURT JUDGEMENT ON SECTION 377

In a historic judgement in 2009, the Delhi High Court 'read down' Section 377 of the Indian Penal Code to exclude consensual sex among adults. That is, adults of the same sex are no longer criminals if they, with mutual consent, have sexual intercourse with one another.[4] Although the court intervention was initiated by an NGO working within the potentially de-politicizing framework of AIDS prevention, when the issue reached court, a number of other more political groups also entered the process, such as Voices Against 377, a broad coalition of feminists, human rights and queer activists. Thus the judgement that resulted, in a sense, reflects the radical transformation in common sense brought about by over a decade of queer politics.

Anchoring the judgement to the Fundamental Rights to life, equality and freedom guaranteed to every citizen, and invoking the inclusiveness envisaged by the Constitution, the judges held:

> In our view, Indian Constitutional law does not permit the statutory criminal law to be held captive by the popular misconceptions of who the LGBTs are. It cannot be forgotten that discrimination is antithesis of equality and that it is the recognition of equality which will foster the dignity of every individual.
>
> We declare that Section 377 IPC, insofar it criminalises consensual sexual acts of adults in private, is violative of Articles 21, 14 and 15 of the Constitution.

Several right-wing groups have appealed this judgement in the Supreme Court, where at the time of going to press, it was pending.

The judgement has given an unprecedented legitimacy to queer identity, in ways that far exceed any limited notion of civil rights of homosexual people. Several legal commentators have pointed out that the Delhi High Court's interpretation of the anti-discrimination provisions of Article 15 could potentially benefit other discriminated-against groups such as disabled persons, religious minorities, and so on.

What is interesting is the general approval for the judgement even in the mainstream—an indicator, as I have already suggested, of the successful shifts in common sense effected by over a decade of queer interventions at every level. Of course, now that Section 377 is on its way out, the fissures and differences within the movement will become more visible. There are those who are content to be gay or lesbian without fear of opprobrium, and don't want to be political at all; there are queer, politically aware people who are Hindu right-wing or pro-capitalist or anti-reservations; and of course, there is queer politics that is opposed to all these. This is the moment of coming of age for queer politics, when it encounters the searing recognition with which feminism has only recently come to terms, that not all non-heterosexual people are queer, just as not all women are feminist; and not all queer people (nor all politically active women) are Left-oriented or secular.

As a friend who is, among other things, a queer activist, put it to me, 'Now that gay is glamorous, the media constantly want me to talk about my gay "lifestyle". But when I say that my work is in urban studies, and I want to talk about slum demolitions, they switch off.'

It is not enough, never enough, to see sexuality issues in terms of a framework of minority rights/privacy/civil liberties, so that the letters of the alphabet (LGBTHK . . .)

continue to proliferate endlessly *outside* the unchallenged heterosexual space.

In the words of Alok Gupta and Arvind Narrain (2010):

> The queer struggle is also about other forms of transgression, such as inter-caste and inter-community relationships which are sought to be curbed by society. What links queer people to couples who love across caste and community lines is the fact that both are exercising their right to love at enormous personal risk and in the process disrupting existing lines of social authority.

The term 'queer' indicates transgressive desire of all sorts, and enables a questioning of the supposed naturalness of the heterosexual identity. If we recognize that 'normal' heterosexuality is painfully constructed and that it is kept in place by a range of cultural, bio-medical and economic controls; and that these controls help sustain existing hierarchies of class and caste and gender, then we would have to accept that all of us are—or have the potential to be—queer.

SEXUAL VIOLENCE

'Manney nyaay chahiye' (I want justice)

A FATE WORSE THAN DEATH?

Consider carefully the term 'rape' and its implications.

Would anybody ever say that rape is acceptable? From the most complacent patriarch to the angriest feminist, all would declare rape to be a terrible crime. But the apparent consensus is mythical, for the reasons behind arriving at this opinion are diametrically opposite. For patriarchal forces, rape is evil because it is a crime against the honour of the family, whereas feminists denounce rape because it is a crime against the autonomy and bodily integrity of a woman. This difference in understanding rape naturally leads to diametrically opposite proposals for fighting rape.

In the patriarchal perspective, rape is a fate worse than death; there is no normal life possible for the raped woman; the way to avoid rape is to lock women up at home, within the family, under patriarchal controls. In this understanding, the raped woman is responsible for the crime against her because either she crossed the *lakshman rekha* of time (by going out after dark) or the *lakshman rekha* of respectability (by dressing in unconventional ways or by leaving the four walls of her home at all).

This patriarchal understanding is pervasive in the judiciary. For example, in 2008, the Chief Justice of Karnataka, Cyriac Joseph, stated that immodest dressing was the cause of the increasing crimes against women:

'Nowadays, women wear such kind of dresses even in temples and churches that when we go to places of worship, instead of meditating on God, we end up meditating on the person before us.'[1] And the Chairperson of the Karnataka State Human Rights Commission said in a public meeting: 'Yes, men are bad . . . But who asked them [the women] to venture out in the night . . . Women should not have gone out in the night and when they do, there is no point in complaining that men touched them and hit them.'[2]

Such a patriarchal understanding of rape is exactly what leads to the remedy sometimes proposed by the courts themselves, of getting the rapist to marry the woman he raped. The marriage is meant to restore social order. Once the rapist is the woman's husband, the act of sex is retrospectively legitimized because of course, the consent of the woman to sex is irrelevant, in marriage and out of it (the Domestic Violence Act of 2005 recognizes marital rape, but the rape laws of the country do not). The morals of Indian society do not permit consensual sex outside marriage, but if you rape a woman, you can marry her!

The existing law on rape, Section 375 of the Indian Penal Code, recognizes only penetration of the vagina by the penis as rape. All other forms of sexual assault are considered as lesser crimes, deserving of a smaller quantum of punishment. Thus, penetration by objects or, in the case of very young girls, by a finger, does not constitute rape. These are covered by sections on 'outraging a woman's modesty' and carry a smaller punishment. A judgment on a case of sexual assault on a baby actually pondered on whether even these sections applied, since it was debatable whether a baby could be said to have developed 'modesty'![3]

Why do all these other acts of violence carry a smaller punishment?

Flavia Agnes argues that this is because rape laws are based on 'the same old notions of chastity, virginity, premium on marriage and fear of female sexuality.' Penis penetration may lead to pregnancies by other men and thus is a greater threat to patrilineal property rights and the patriarchal power structure, than other kinds of sexual and non-sexual assaults on women. It is in keeping with this understanding of rape, she points out, that in all other criminal offences, injury and hurt caused by weapons is considered more grievous, deserving of greater punishment than that caused by limbs; but in the case of sexual assault, injury caused by iron rods, bottles or sticks is considered to be a lesser crime (1992).

Revealingly, the other crime that does carry the same severity of punishment as 'rape' is anal penetration by the penis, despite the consent of both parties. Section 377, as we have seen, criminalizes consensual anal penetration, even in a heterosexual relationship. What links the two? We have talked of 'legitimate procreative sexuality' earlier—well, there's your answer. Section 375 protects patrilineal descent and property systems; Section 377 punishes a greater threat to the social order—the possibility of escaping compulsory heterosexuality altogether.

The feminist understanding of rape proceeds on completely different premises. While recognizing rape as a serious crime, its harm is seen to lie in the attack on a woman's autonomy and bodily integrity. Feminists reject the idea that it's a fate worse than death. If feminist campaigns against sexual harassment and sexual assault could be summed up in one slogan, it would be this: **Stop blaming the victim.**

In the feminist view, the raped woman does not lose her honour, the rapist does. For instance, the campaign against the rapists of Bhanwari Devi coined the slogan *Izzat gayi kis ki, Bhateri Bhateri ki,* meaning it was not Bhanwari Devi who lost her honour, but the village defending the rapists. Bhanwari Devi—this Dalit woman who was raped by upper-caste men as a punishment for trying to implement the government's law against child marriage in her village—is a heroine for the movement. Bhanwari Devi is the dignified and public face of the campaign against sexual violence against women.

Prompt redress is essential, feminists hold, for checking sexual violence of all sorts. But this is precisely what the Indian justice system does not offer.

SEXIST COURTROOMS

Alleged rapists are routinely acquitted for 'lack of evidence', and proven rapists often given a reduced sentence, sympathetically citing their youth and the promising life ahead of them. Gratuitous references to 'Western women' and their supposed attitudes to sex can be found in formal judgements as well as in statements on rape by officials.

A 1983 judgement of the Gujarat High Court made the progressive argument that corroborative evidence for a charge of rape was not necessary in general, and that a woman's complaint of rape should be taken on its own merits. But it justified this argument on very patriarchal grounds. It held that Indian society—unlike the permissive West—is tradition-bound and, therefore, a woman was unlikely to make a false accusation of rape as she would 'be reluctant to admit that any incident which is likely to reflect on her chastity' had occurred. Western women, it was implied, are more than capable of such things.*

The Gujarat High Court judgment went on to qualify its position by elaborating on the circumstances in which corroboration may be insisted upon. That is, when an adult woman 'is found in a compromising position', it is possible that 'there is likelihood of her having levelled such an accusation on account of the instinct of self-preservation'. In other words, if the tradition-bound society of India made 'innocent' women reluctant to level false accusations of rape, it would, at the same time, motivate 'promiscuous' women to hide their lack of virtue precisely through such accusations.

So, whose innocence or guilt is on trial here? In rape cases, always that of the woman it seems, never that of the alleged rapist.

In another episode from Gujarat (in 2009), a British woman living in India, who charged an Indian man with raping her, was humiliated during the trial and broke down completely. She has made a formal complaint to the Chief Justice of the Gujarat High Court after a defence

---

* As a chief minister of Kerala said during a furore over the rape of female tourists, 'There is no need to make such a fuss, rape in the US is as common as drinking a cup of tea.' See http://www.rediff.com/news/1996/2308ek. htm.

lawyer asked her a series of 'irrelevant questions designed to question my character'. In front of a packed court of jeering men, the twenty-three-year-old was asked whether she drank alcohol, socialized with men and even how often she took a shower. All the while, the man she had accused of assaulting her sat just a few feet away.[4]

Two female officers of the Indian armed forces who, at different times (in 2005 and 2009), accused their senior officers of 'physical and mental harassment' and sexual harassment, respectively, were court-martialled and dishonourably discharged from service. They claimed their charges were never investigated, but were pushed under the carpet.[5] One of them committed suicide six years later.[6]

A rape convict cleared the civil service exam in 2010 while serving his sentence, and was deemed by the Delhi High Court to have 'redeemed himself in jail', his incarceration of five years having met with 'the ends of justice'. His victim, who committed suicide, is beyond justice or redemption, and the Court was not interested in her. While tutoring her in chemistry, her suicide note had said, he drugged her, had sex with her and later blackmailed her into continuing to have sex with him, promising her that they would soon get married. He then tried to make her have sex with a third person from whom he wanted a favour. After this, she committed suicide. However, according to the news report, 'The High Court found no evidence to substantiate this allegation (in the suicide note) that the woman actually had sex with a third person'. So his conviction under Section 306 (abetment to suicide) has been set aside, and he is deemed to have served his sentence for 'obtaining sex on the false promise of marriage', which constitutes rape in our legal system.[7]*

So, look out for the bright young bureaucrat, Ashok Rai, 'alias Amit'—the skills he showed as a young tutor will be multiplied with the power that comes with being a *sarkari afsar*. The fact that he 'cracked' the 'tough civils', makes our judiciary look indulgently upon his boyish pranks— drugging, raping and pimping. He is now well equipped to take up the reins of the country's administration.

Bhanwari Devi, fifteen years after the incident, still awaits the hearing of her appeal against the acquittal of her upper-caste rapists by the Rajasthan High Court. '*Manne nyaay chahiye* (I want justice)', she declared simply at a meeting honouring her in Delhi, to a thunderous standing ovation.

The current rape laws are thus very problematic from the feminist point of view, and there are on-going debates among feminists and democratic rights groups on the kinds of amendments required. One important suggestion is to remove the narrowly-defined 'rape' and replace it with a series of degrees of 'sexual assault', the punishment increasing in severity with the degree of physical harm caused. With the possible repeal of Section 377 on the cards, gender neutrality with regard to the victim is being strongly

---

* Correction: It can constitute rape if so interpreted by judges. There have also been cases in which judges have ruled otherwise. A 1984 judgment of the Calcutta High Court sternly ruled that 'If a fully grown girl consents to sexual intercourse on the promise of marriage and continues to indulge in such activity until she becomes pregnant, it is an act of promiscuity.' And promiscuity, we know, is a Western aberration far more serious than mere rape.

proposed, so that rapes of men, boys and *hijras*, too, can be taken into account. The perpetrator is generally male but, in cases of custodial rape or rape in the context of a clear power situation, gender neutrality is also being proposed for the perpetrator. This last suggestion is very contentious within the feminist perspective though, as there is a fear that gender neutrality with regard to the perpetrator, except in clearly defined situations such as custody/authority, will only further make women the target of the law rather than offer them protection, given our overwhelmingly patriarchal and sexist context.

SEXUAL HARASSMENT AT THE WORKPLACE

Sexual harassment at the workplace was recognized by a landmark judgment of the Supreme Court (1997, Vishakha vs. State of Rajasthan) that laid down guidelines for all employers to protect women employees from sexual harassment. The judgment declared sexual harassment at the workplace to be a violation of the fundamental rights to life, equality and the right to practise any profession, as guaranteed in the Constitution. The guidelines defined various dimensions of sexual harassment in terms of 'unwelcome' conduct of specific kinds, the operative notion being that of consent. The Court also specified the composition of the complaints committees. The moving force behind these guidelines was the intervention of several feminist NGOs and women's groups after the rape of Bhanwari Devi, who was raped as punishment for carrying out government-sanctioned work, as we have seen. In the years since these guidelines, several universities have come up with carefully-formulated sexual harassment codes, as have some NGOs and some private-sector employers. The codes put in place by the latter two kinds of organizations are uneven in character, depending on the presence within the organization of feminists with a perspective on sexual harassment. Where such a perspective is lacking, the committees and policy become just one more employer-generated disciplinary mechanism against employees, especially since, in most such cases, there are no trade unions.

SOME UNIVERSITY EXPERIENCES

University policies (for instance, at Delhi University; Jawaharlal Nehru University, Delhi; North-Eastern Hill University, Shillong), have tended to arise from existing democratic politics in the university community. The Supreme Court guidelines acted as a catalyst to focus the energies of progressive political groupings on campuses and of individual teachers and students towards the formulation of appropriate codes and implementation mechanisms. In an academic environment, the definition of sexual harassment would have to be different from other kinds of workplaces. Universities are filled with young people in their formative years, and we need to think about what it does to them when teachers routinely express derogatory opinions about women. ('What does it matter what grade you get, you only have to get married anyway?' 'Women are generally irrational'. Both these are statements that have actually been made by male professors in the classroom.) Equally problematic are apparent compliments to women students, and sexually-loaded comments. The greatest danger is that routine interaction of this sort normalizes an environment of harassment and naturalizes sexualized forms of interaction between teachers and students. The fact that professors control grades, jobs and promotions makes students and younger colleagues especially vulnerable.

It is not necessary that each such instance be formally addressed. We can work to empower students not to accept such behaviour, and to make it socially unacceptable. But there will be instances where the situation cannot be handled informally, and there will be instances of more serious sexual misconduct, such as quid pro quo sexual advances for jobs or grades.

At least in the three universities I have listed earlier, the codes that were put in place resulted from long processes of mobilization and discussion at several levels, co-ordinated by people thrown up by the campaigns, often in the teeth of opposition from university authorities, but eventually installed within university policy due to the strength of the struggles. These kinds of movements are characteristic of university campuses in India, bringing together a range of political groupings over specific issues. They are broad fronts that are leaderless; they are an expression of direct democracy, and the very real differences in political perspectives among the constituents are set aside in the coming together over that specific issue. Such mobilizations are necessarily time-bound, and they dissipate after some sort of resolution is reached.

The policies of Delhi University (DU) and Jawaharlal

Nehru University (JNU) are reasonably flexible and take into account local specificities and requirements. For instance, the DU policy introduced a mix of elected and nominated members on committees to balance out the requirements of democracy with the recognition that, since sexual harassment arises from a context of widely prevalent misogyny and patriarchal attitudes, elections may well return candidates who reflect that value system. The definition of sexual harassment and the constitution of committees are fine-tuned to the academic context; punishments are carefully graded rather than vindictively punitive, since making sexual harassment visible is also meant to produce new norms of acceptable behaviour; and the implementation is by the University, not by a remote authority with no sense of the local context. The composition of committees reflects and draws upon the university community, while incorporating an 'outside' element through nomination, as required by the Vishakha guidelines.

Our experience has been that university authorities are notoriously resistant to recognizing sexual harassment as an issue, especially when it involves harassment of students and junior colleagues by senior professors. The successful carrying through of a complaint, from its first being lodged to punishment being meted out, almost never smoothly follows the due process established by policies. Particularly at the stage after a committee has submitted its report, its implementation is often stalled indefinitely by university authorities and, all the while, the sexual harasser continues to wield power over the complainant and his/her supporters.

A CASE STUDY

Here's a fairly representative case study. In 2006, a complaint was lodged against a male professor of Delhi University by a woman in an administrative post. This professor was extremely powerful at that time and held several university positions. Once it was learnt that a complaint had been filed, several students and colleagues came forward to testify that his behaviour was routinely offensive and sexually loaded towards women—much as in the case of Dominique Strauss-Kahn, to whom we will return later. A properly instituted committee found him guilty and recommended certain relatively minor punishments—largely, his removal from positions of power for a period of three years. This report was not formally tabled in the manner required to implement it and it languished in the vice chancellor's office, despite an RTI application[8] by the primary complainant, which was refused under Section 8 (g)—that the disclosure of the information 'would endanger the life or physical safety of a person'! Under a wide range of pressures from the university community, including large-scale lobbying at different levels with the administration, publicity in the media, and demonstrations and protests, the report was finally tabled and the punishment carried out.

Immediately, the professor moved court against the University; the university authorities, not interested in winning the case,* often did not even appear at hearings; and finally, the professor's lawyer obtained a ruling from the Supreme Court that the inquiry procedure had not followed 'natural justice' in that the accused had not had

---

* Rather, the opposite!

the opportunity to cross-examine the witnesses. If the University had been interested in taking the matter seriously, its lawyers could have made a legitimate argument that there is a legal precedent to rule out cross-examination in sexual harassment cases where the accused is powerful, because of the intimidation of the witnesses that is made possible by this. At any rate, following the court directive, the inquiry was then duly reopened at the point of cross-examination, and the accused was permitted to send lists of questions to all the witnesses, including the primary complainant. By this time, the latter had left the university and even the country, while the professor stalked its corridors arrogantly.*

The questions framed by the professor and his lawyer were textbook cases of sexual harassment in themselves. Each faculty member who had testified against him, as well as the primary complainant, was asked dozens of crudely worded questions about his or her private life and the relationships he or she had ever had. The irrelevance of this information to the charge against him was breathtakingly obvious. Nevertheless, each of the questionnaires was duly completed, and the matter went back, as directed by the Court, to the university committee, which then submitted its report in 2009. Till today, that report has not been formally tabled by the vice chancellor. One wonders if the report would have been suppressed again had it cleared the professor of the charges against him.

Meanwhile, the professor planted stories in the media, falsely claiming that his innocence was established by the Court, and not one reporter who was thus primed sought a

---

* He was even sent abroad on a government-sponsored prestigious fellowship.

clarification from the Court itself, or from any other party concerned.

This is a typical incident in terms of the process and the struggle but, of course, there are also instances in which sexual harassment policies have succeeded in obtaining justice for the complainant. Even in the case detailed above, sexual harassment as such and what constitutes it, has acquired visibility and been acknowledged.

DANGERS OF PROPOSED CENTRAL LEGISLATION

This limited degree of success on some university campuses in naming sexual harassment and dealing with it, is now threatened in my opinion, by a proposed Central legislation, the Bill on the Protection of Women Against Sexual Harassment at Workplace 2010.

Women's organizations have pointed out a serious problem with this Bill, that it makes punishable 'false and malicious complaints' of sexual harassment. This is opposed to the spirit of the Vishakha judgment that had held that no action should be taken against the complainant even if the complaint is not upheld. This was meant to ensure that women could feel secure in making a complaint even against powerful people at their workplace. Also, a complaint may end up not being upheld only for lack of evidence. It is important to remember that *all* laws can be misused—people are often falsely implicated in murder charges or in charges of financial irregularity. But this does not lead to initiatives to remove laws on murder and theft from the statute books!

On the whole though, women's groups have welcomed the Bill and asked for its speedy passing. Once passed, the status of different existing policies at different workplaces is uncertain.

I believe that no country-level legislation, even a feminist-drafted alternative, can be sensitive to the specificities of sexual harassment in different work contexts, from university to factory floor, from office to construction site. We have seen how difficult it is to spell out what sexual harassment is, even within a relatively homogeneous work space like a university. One overarching definition for all workplaces is bound to miss out on the slippery, ambiguous and locally-specific modes of sexual harassment. The possibility of justice is greater when small work-based communities hammer out acceptable norms of behaviour and punishment that are appropriate to it. More importantly, such a self-constituting community is more likely to be active and to constitute itself anew constantly, thus resulting in suitable amendments from time to time in the policy.

On the other hand, the problem with law is that unless it is very broad in scope, it permits innumerable loopholes; but if too broad, it can either be ineffective or draconian, drawing into its ambit a number of ambiguous situations. Thus, an ineffective but draconian law on sexual harassment may be on the verge of replacing university and other workplace-generated policies, carefully modulated to local specificities.

'FALSE COMPLAINTS'

It is worth returning to the 'false complaint' scenario, particularly as it arose recently with two high-profile cases of sexual harassment, against Wikileaks founder Julian Assange and IMF chief Dominique Strauss-Kahn. In both cases it has been alleged that these men have been targeted for their anti-establishment politics. And in both cases, the supposed progressive nature of their politics has been used to cast doubt on the complainants.

In the case of Assange, his supporters allege that his sexual encounters with the two complainants was consensual, taking the form of sexual harassment complaints only afterwards, under pressure from powerful governments affected by the Wikileaks disclosures. However, in the Swedish warrant for his arrest, both his accusers conceded that they had had separate consensual sexual encounters with Assange, which became non-consensual specifically after he refused to use a condom or replace a broken one. This constitutes sexual harassment under Swedish law. That is, consent may be given for specific levels and types of sexual activity, not once and for all, not for anything and everything. Assange (if found guilty) should be punished in accordance with Swedish law for non-consensual sex within an initially consensual encounter.*

---

* This is not even recognized as a crime in the US where the clamour for his punishment is the highest—Sarah Palin urged the US administration to 'Hunt down the WikiLeaks chief like the Taliban'. Prominent US politician Mike Huckabee called for his execution on Fox News programme, while Fox News commentator Bob Beckel, referring to Assange, publicly called for people to 'illegally shoot the son of a bitch'.

Without giving him a clean chit in advance then, the question that some feminists are raising is whether the international hunt for him and the punishment he is currently undergoing, are commensurate with the possible crime. Questioning the 'unusual zeal' in pursuing the rape allegations against Assange, the spokesperson for Women Against Rape[9] pointed out that, in Sweden, up to 90 per cent of reported rapes do not, in fact, get to court. Defending both the right of the rape victims to anonymity and the right of the defendants to be presumed innocent until proven guilty, the statement criticizes the fact that Assange, with no previous criminal convictions, was refused bail in England when in other cases, bail following rape allegations is routine. The statement concludes:

> There is a long tradition of the use of rape and sexual assault for political agendas that have nothing to do with women's safety . . . Women don't take kindly to our demand for safety being misused, while rape continues to be neglected at best or protected at worst.[10]

Our feminism requires us to raise feminist issues within every space, as also to recognize when feminist struggles are sought to be appropriated by the most patriarchal of forces. We need to insist that feminist battles be fought by feminists, not by those using feminism for anti-feminist ends. Assange should be punished according to Swedish laws on sexual harassment, if found guilty after a trial, but feminist responsibility is equally great to ensure that he is not punished beyond the requirements of his crime.

'Consent' is not some easily definable thing that can be assumed once and for all. One can give consent to some kinds of sexual activity and not to others; one can give consent to a sexual relationship and then not want to have sex at some point in that relationship; one can give consent to sex with a condom, and not want sex without it; one can insist that within a consensual sexual relationship, if the condom broke, both parties should undergo HIV testing for the safety of both partners. These notions of consent are not 'legal' everywhere, especially in India, fortunately for Indian men. As it happens, in Sweden, the refusal to recognize any of the above legally constitutes sexual harassment.

The supposed weakening of the case against Dominique Strauss-Kahn is equally murky. The hotel maid who has alleged that he forced her to perform oral sex on him has been put under the scanner for every lie she has told as an immigrant worker with a precarious status—misrepresenting her income to qualify for housing; claiming a friend's child as hers to increase her tax refund; misrepresenting her situation at home in Guinea in order to get asylum. None of these has any bearing on her complaint of sexual harassment. In addition, the usual kinds of doubts have been cast on her testimony: Why did she wait to make her complaint rather than complain immediately? Why are there minor discrepancies between the sequence of events as she reported them initially (that she waited in the hallway till Strauss-Kahn left his room, and immediately complained), and later (that she cleaned another room after the incident, returned to Strauss-Kahn's room to clean it, and only then did she complain). While all these details have been dredged up and pored over by the media, a similar dredging up of Strauss-Kahn's history would reveal information more pertinent to this case—the fact that several other women have now come forward to establish his long history of violent sexual assaults.

Of course, as argued earlier, the in-built feature of any law or policy, whether on sexual harassment or murder or financial irregularity, is that it can be 'misused'. And so it is entirely possible that some complaints of sexual harassment may indeed be false and motivated by external political alignments. But even in the event that a patently false complaint is made against a person of known probity, all we can do is to insist on an immediate and time-bound inquiry.

ONLY GOOD WOMEN DESERVE PROTECTION

Sexual violence is only the most visible aspect of a general climate of misogyny in which all women are always under the scanner for signs of immoral behaviour.

Every woman knows that the positions marked 'good woman' and 'bad woman', *susheel aurat* and *baazaru aurat*, madonna and whore, are not stable and fixed. Every woman lives in the constant knowledge of how easy it is to fall from the light side into the dark side, and how impossible it is, once fallen, ever to get back again into the light. An unthinking gesture, a careless physical movement, the wrong kind of dress in a public place or in the home, and suddenly, that's it! You're exposed as a prostitute.

As a Malaysian feminist wrote on her blog:

> When sex workers are raped because of their profession, *all* women and girls are implicated in this act of violence. How? Sex workers are assaulted and abused because they are viewed as 'damaged goods' or sex objects who do not deserve society's respect. This means that all women and girls have to be careful about how they behave and dress, because the line between 'pure' and 'slutty' blurs and changes beyond our control and exposes us to a similar abuse perpetrated against sex workers.[11]

'Prostitute' becomes an easily available general insult, suggesting someone willing to be bought, a person with no ethics; hence, politics and parliament are routinely compared to prostitution by different political strands. But it is most directly applicable to women making themselves visible in public spaces, potentially destabilizing the patriarchal social order. In both cases, the insult arises from the comparison to a woman who, of her own will, has sex with many men outside all prescribed social rules; as opposed to the non-prostitute woman, who has sex only under conditions strictly controlled by patriarchy.

Let us look at four recent instances of this kind of labelling and the feminist responses to it.

UNMARRIED WOMAN/WIDOW/PROSTITUTE

During the state assembly elections in West Bengal in 2011, in which Mamata Banerjee's party roundly defeated the CPI(M), a senior CPI(M) leader, Anil Basu, linked a familiar line of attack—alleging 'foreign funds'—to Mamata

Banerjee's sexual probity when he said that like any woman from Sonagachhi (Kolkata's 'red light area'), Mamata would not even look at smaller clients now that she had a big client, the US, to finance her campaign.[12] There was also a reference by another CPI(M) member to the parting in Mamata's hair that has never known red (the red *sindur* or vermilion in the parting of a woman's hair signifying marriage in many parts of India), which explained, he said, her enmity towards the red of communism.[13]

The porous borders evident here between the categories of 'unmarried woman', 'widow' and 'prostitute'—each of them a woman unbound by marriage—reflects the intense patriarchal anxiety about controlling female sexuality. This is a broader phenomenon—in Kannada, Tamil and Telugu, 'widow' is a term of abuse (for men too) and in some North Indian languages, the words for 'widow' and 'prostitute' are either very similar or identical. In Hindi, for instance, *raand* is widow as well as prostitute. The idea of sexual desire in widows is till today, as threatening as it was in 19th century Bengal, about which Tanika Sarkar writes in her aptly titled essay, "Wicked Widows" (2009). Accompanying this expectation of sexual purity on the part of widows and simultaneous fears about their sexual agency, is of course, the sexual exploitation of widows, often by men of their own families, which is never acknowledged or punished.

In the face of widespread outrage over Anil Basu's comments, the Party stepped in to censure him, saying that it is reprehensible to question a woman's chastity in the course of a political campaign. In other words, Basu had violated the code of patriarchy by calling a woman unchaste, a term that is an insult in the vocabulary of patriarchy. But suppose a sex worker from Sonagachhi were to contest elections, would attacking her as unchaste be justified? It is when the only acceptable role of a woman is that of a mother, a daughter or a daughter-in-law that 'whore' becomes an insult.

After becoming chief minister, Mamata Banerjee herself has more than once taken patriarchal and misogynist stands on rape and on women, which only further illustrates the fact that these ways of seeing the world do not spare those who are subordinated by it.

But then, what is a *feminist* way of understanding and responding to being called a whore? Perhaps another controversy will take us closer to an answer.

CHHINAAL

The eminent Hindi (male) writer, Vibhuti Narain Rai, said in an interview with a Hindi journal that revealing autobiographies by women writers in Hindi were merely a celebration of promiscuity (*bewafaai*), and that it seemed they were competing with one another to prove which of them was the biggest slut (*chhinaal*) of all. The word *chhinaal* refers to a promiscuous woman, an adulteress. While strictly speaking, it is not a word used for prostitute, it is comparable to the looser meanings of 'slut' in English. *Bewafaai* literally means disloyalty but in this context, it refers to women having sexual encounters outside marriage, that is, being promiscuous. Much of the storm of response tended to whirl around Rai's supposedly calling women writers prostitutes, and around whether *chhinaal* does, in fact, mean prostitute (Vijay 2010).

Feminist Hindi writer Archana Verma however,

highlighted what, for me, is the key issue—that the very notion of sexual fidelity is suspect, especially in the context of male-female relations, in which the expectation of fidelity is always one-sided:

> Infidelity was born on the day that natural flows of sexual desire were bound into the legal and formal permanence of marriage; and in the process of ensuring male control over progeny and property, women were chained with the fetters of fidelity (2010).[14]

What has happened now, says Verma, is merely that the woman writer has finally broken faith with the conspiracy of silence invoking shame and honour, in which she had fully participated—an enemy to her own self. In the privacy of the internal courtyard of the home, Verma notes, women have long sung songs that expressed illicit desire, uttered the names of their intimate body parts and their bodily flows, and raged about the violence and the betrayal that were their burden to bear. But the literary form of the autobiography bursts out of that courtyard and frontally assaults masculinist middle-class sensibilities right there, in the public domain. Archana Verma accepts as a badge of honour, the term *bewafaa*, which she takes to mean unfaithful to this patriarchal ideology. But that *bewafaai is baawafaa* (faithful) to something else—a commitment to her own sense of self.

Women find themselves arguing futilely that 'just because' I go out to work/smoke/drink/wear unorthodox clothes/enjoy male company—that doesn't make me a whore. Is there any comparable good/bad imagery for men?

Of course not. The feminist response to being called whores or *chhinaal* should not be to protest fruitlessly, 'We are not whores!' but to turn the insult around and ask, 'What makes you think this is an insult? We refuse the terms of this insult.' What if all women were to say we *are* 'loose'—we are not tightly controlled—and if that makes us whores, then we are all whores. If we are all bad women, then patriarchy had better watch out.

Or, as Archana Verma puts it: 'One day, I will hear hurled at me the words, loose woman, *chhinaal*, prostitute . . . And I will turn around and say, "Thank you for the compliment". That day will come. And it will be a day of feminist celebration.'

CHADDIS ARE PINK

There have been other feminist responses along these lines to other provocations, too. In 2009, men of a hitherto little-known Hindu right-wing organization, called Sri Ram Sene, physically attacked young women in pubs in the city of Mangalore. These attacks, supposedly an attempt to protect Indian culture from defilement by Western values, were met with protests and solidarity campaigns all over the country, but the most imaginative one came to be called the Pink Chaddi campaign. A cheeky Facebook group was launched by Delhi journalist Nisha Susan, under the name of 'Consortium of Pub-going, Loose and Forward Women', which called upon women to send pink *chaddis* (underwear) to the leader of the Sri Ram Sene, Pramod Muthalik, as a gift on Valentine's Day, in a non-violent gesture of ridicule and protest. Over 2000 chaddis were in fact delivered to the Sri Ram Sene office, and the organization was a butt of ridicule across the world. It is striking that the campaign used the word 'chaddi' rather than 'panty', simultaneously desexualizing the piece of clothing, ungendering it (chaddi refers to underwear in general, not just to women's panties), and playing on the pejorative slang for Hindu right-wingers, after the uniform of their parent organization, the RSS, whose members wear khaki shorts. Although it was at one level an undoubtedly successful campaign, it faced criticism from conservative quarters for obvious reasons, and also from the Left of the political spectrum.

The latter chastised the campaign for élitism ('after all, only westernized women in cities go to pubs') and for diverting attention to such a trivial issue when, for most women in India, their very survival was at stake. Is going to pubs what feminism is about, was the question such critics raised. Of course not. Nor had the Consortium claimed it was anything as large as 'feminism' itself. It was a specific campaign in response to a specific attack and, as Nisha Susan put it, 'for many of those who signed up, neither Valentine's Day nor pub-going meant anything. What we agreed on is the need to end violence in the name of somebody's idea of Indian culture' (2009). The campaign brazenly owned up to the identities which the Hindu right-wing attributed to women in pubs—'loose and forward'—and wore them as badges of pride. And it clearly touched a chord across the country, for most people understood it as defiance against moral policing by the Hindu Right in general, not as merely about women's right to drink in pubs.

BESHARAM!

The most recent instance of reclaiming sexist insults was the organizing of Slut Walks in Delhi and Bhopal. Slut Walks must be understood as a critique of the victim-blaming culture that surrounds rape. The original Slut Walk was a reaction to a Canadian police officer's remark that if women dress 'like sluts', they must expect to be raped. However, the overwhelmingly positive responses world-wide to Slut Walks revealed that blaming the victim was not an attitude restricted to the West.

In India, within the feminist camp, misgivings were expressed that the English word 'slut' has no resonance at all here. In response, the organizers of the march added a Hindi phrase explaining the name, so that it became Slut Walk, *arthaat Besharmi Morcha*, drawing on the Hindi word *besharam* meaning 'without shame', shameless, often used for women who refuse to live by patriarchal rules. What was interesting about Slut Walks in India (held in Bhopal and Delhi in July 2011) was that they were not organized by the established women's movement organizations and well-known feminist faces, but by much younger women new to political organizing, who were expressing, however, an old and powerful feminist demand—the right to safety in public spaces.

As Pratiksha Baxi (2011) put it:

It is really very simple. In India, for women to reclaim their rights whatever their class, caste or community, amounts to attracting the allegation of being *without shame*. Surely we have all been *besharam* for a good part of our lifetimes, and one would hope that we will continue to be—as long as being autonomous continues to mean being *besharam* in our culture?

Slut Walk *arthaat Besharmi Morcha* must be recognized as only the latest episode in a long history in India, of women militantly taking to the streets against sexual violence— from the late 1970s when women's groups mobilized around a Supreme Court judgment acquitting the police rapists of a young tribal girl Mathura, and against the gang rape of Rameeza Bi by policemen in Hyderabad in 1978; to the 1990s, demanding justice for Bhanwari Devi; to innumerable demonstrations and protests in towns and cities and on university campuses all over the country that take place from time to time, against incidents of molestation, harassment and rape. It is a very long, very powerful history of struggle and an amazing, inspiring legacy that we have inherited.

WHY IS RAPE OUR GREATEST FEAR?

As feminists, we walk a tightrope on the question of rape. On the one hand, we want the recognition that rape is only one end of a spectrum of violence, at the other end of which is a range of male behaviour that in India, is endearingly called 'Eve teasing'. We want recognition that the pervasiveness of such a misogynist culture severely restricts women's access to public spaces. We want recognition that not every woman has to be actually raped for her to learn to restrict her own movements—the belief that the threat of rape is everywhere, that it can happen at any time, that it is the worst fate that can befall women, is enough to make us police ourselves and restrict our own mobility.

But on the other hand, feminists also want to demystify rape, to begin to see it not as a unique and life-destroying form of violation from which one can never recover, but as (merely) another kind of violence against persons, many of whom could be men. The fact that men too, are raped is rarely acknowledged, because of the dominant perception that it is only women who are perpetually violable and in danger of rape. This silence around male rape magnifies the shame and trauma of the raped man, reduced and feminized by the act; and simultaneously produces only women as eternally rapeable (Mookherjee 2011; Stemple 2009).

Hence our preference for the term rape *survivor* rather than rape *victim*. Does the real damage of 'rape' lie in the web of meanings around it rather than in the act itself? 'Sexual' violence has a potency that is greater than the actual violence of the act or the physical damage inflicted. People recover even from murderous assaults, but once identified as 'sexual', the significance of even a less physically damaging attack is radically transformed; the shame, the terror and the pain of the victim are that much more magnified. Sexual assault has been so constructed that it is the most feared, most terrifying and most humiliating form of attack. A booklet written by a feminist activist mentions 'the paralysing effect on a young girl' that 'the sight of an erect penis can in itself have.' This feeling of paralysis and horror in the face of an attack recognized as sexual is not restricted to women.

A counsellor in Britain heading Survivors, the principal counselling service for male rape survivors, says that even 'big guys' 'freeze' when they are victims of a sexual attack. They talk of being literally unable to move, unable to offer any resistance.

Even without physical violence, sometimes with no physical contact, 'sexual' performances in which people are involved against their will are traumatic in a way in which other encounters are not: such as lewd stares and gestures in public places.

Can this explosive impact of sexual violence on its victims be explained entirely by the empirically verifiable physical acts that constitute it? Or does the impact and maybe even the sexual violence itself, flow from the discourse which constructs 'sex', 'sexual violence' and 'sexuality' as the deepest aspects of one's 'real' and 'private' self, so that the violation of the sense of wholeness in this area threatens one's belief in one's unique selfhood?

This mystification of sexuality as the truest, deepest expression of selfhood is what we must contest. As we have seen, the very idea of rape as violation is located within a patriarchal and patrilineal discourse. We need to free ourselves from the very meaning of rape as the most deadly of all forms of violence, to build up immunity to this virus— the *fear of potential rape*.

This is why we contend that the more the women are out at night and in secluded places, the safer the night and those spaces become for women. I am reminded here of a student's retort to a teacher's claim during a workshop, that women are sexually harassed because they wear jeans.* The student, speaking in Hindi, and clearly not from an upper-class background, said she had found that when she wore *salwar-kameez* she faced more sexual harassment than she did when she wore jeans. Her assessment? That when she was in the former dress, she appeared *seedhi-saadhi* and timid, and unlikely to object, while in jeans, she appeared confident and bold, and therefore men thought twice before taking her on!

RISK AS EMPOWERING

Statistics show that women are more likely to face violence inside their homes than outside; while in public, it is men who face more actual violent behaviour (from other men). Despite this, it is women who are advised to stay home, while there are no restrictions on men moving about in public. Clearly this has to do with two related assumptions: that women face sexual violence only from strangers outside the home; and that sexual violence is a unique and irreparable form of violence. Feminists reject this framework altogether. It is in this context that the idea of the *risk-taking subject* has emerged in feminist thought, in opposition to the *vulnerable subject* (Agnes 2006; Phadke 2007).

Flavia Agnes makes her argument in the context of women's decisions to migrate, and we will come to it in the last chapter. Here, in the context of sexual violence, Shilpa

---

* The Western woman's dress, signifying loose morals!

Phadke suggests that a feminist demand for equal access to public space must be based not on a demand for safety and protection, but on the basis of 'equality of risk'—the recognition that both men and women risk dangers of various kinds. So the feminist project should not be to protect women from attack, which is bound to feed into a narrative enforcing 'safe' behaviour on the part of women themselves. Rather, the goal should be the certainty that if they are attacked, they would receive prompt redress, thus establishing the unequivocal rights of women to be in public spaces at all times of the day and night. What the idea of 'risk' does in the feminist understanding is, it challenges the idea that women should live in a pervasive culture of fear, and rather, emphasizes that in their actual lives, women continuously surmount fear. The poorer and more marginal they are, the more they take inescapable risks without the luxury of thinking too much about it. From this perspective, feminist politics must emphasize the agency of women, and demystify sexual violence as merely one of the many risks faced by people. This attempt to legitimize risk-taking must, of course, says Phadke, be accompanied by putting pressure on the State to provide infrastructure so that women have the option to choose risk-taking behaviour rather than having risk forced on them at every step—for instance, safe public transport at all hours, a network of well-lit public toilets for women, and so on.

After all, isn't a woman engaging in risky behaviour every time she laughs loudly and unselfconsciously in public, loiters without intent, casually maps the world with her stride? That is the kind of risk to which we lay claim.

RAPE AS A POLITICAL WEAPON

Apart from individual or private acts of misogynist violence, feminists have been concerned with sexual violence as a weapon of war, and as part of a wider repertoire of race, communal and caste violence. In India, custodial sexual violence against women (by the police and the army) and the culpability and impunity of the State, have been addressed in significant ways.

In July 2004, a group of women in the capital of the north-eastern state of Manipur militantly protested naked in front of the base of the Indian Army at Kangla Fort, raising a banner with the contemptuous challenge, 'Indian Army Rape Us'. They were protesting the rape, torture and murder of Thangjam Manorama, who was picked up from her home at night by a regiment of Assam Rifles, and whose bullet-ridden and tortured body was found later. Large parts of India are effectively under army rule, the north-eastern states and Kashmir, in particular, being covered by the Armed Forces (Special Powers) Act.[15] From time to time, acts of sexual violence on women (activists as well as relatives of men suspected to be militants) are carried out by members of the Indian State's armed forces.

Mass rape is often used as part of the repressive measures unleashed by the State to crush movements of tribal people, peasants, workers, and political dissidents. It is also common for the rural landed élite to use rape to stifle assertions of the rural poor in sharecropping disputes, reclaiming lost land, or in demanding the payment of minimum wages (Chakravarti 1982). We may remind ourselves that Bhanwari Devi was raped in a political act of vengeance. Sexual violence on women is a weapon in the war on Dalits by the upper castes and by the Hindu Right against minorities, most recently and notably in the pogrom against Muslims in Gujarat in 2002.

Many such instances come to the notice of democratic rights groups and feminists, and are investigated by them, and protested in various ways. Many remain unknown. But for the women's movement in India, the recognition of rape as a political weapon is a significant part of its politics.

'GOVERNANCE FEMINISM'

In the international context however, there is another, disturbing dimension to feminist recognition of rape as a political weapon, drawn to our attention by Janet Halley (2011). In a study of Western (mainly American) feminist intervention in the question of rapes during war, especially in the context of Yugoslavia and Rwanda, Halley notes that the legal agenda started out as a fairly simple commitment to prohibit rape in war and prosecute it vigorously. But gradually, the feminists doing this work moved into an understanding that rape was not merely one of the tools in inter-group warfare but part of 'a global war against women.' Halley terms as 'feminist universalism', the idea that

> women are not a particular group of humanity but a universe of their own. In the new feminist universalist world view, a rape committed during armed conflict was wrongly described as a persecution based on political, racial or religious grounds, even when the armed conflict had broken out over political, racial or religious divisions . . . This idea was operationalized in a provision of the Rome

Statute which allows the prosecution of a new crime against humanity, namely, persecution based on gender.

Thus, the ethno-nationalist conflict in the Balkans, for instance, becomes 'a war against women', without any acknowledgement that men, too, were tortured and killed in it. Thus, the specificities of politics in different locations are erased, and it is assumed that all conflict anywhere can be translated as part of the global 'war on women' as understood by white American feminists. It is assumed that women have common interests across all other identities.

Halley and her colleagues term this kind of intervention 'governance feminism' (Halley et al. 2006), a development in which a certain strand of feminism has entered the corridors of international power. This is a white universalist, top-down, State-centred feminism. From our location in the non-West, we cannot help but recognize this feminism as an ally of the new world order and the new imperialism which use the language of women's rights to protect their strategic interests. Such feminist initiatives arise from international NGOs which are influential in the power structures of Western States, and have little or nothing to with social movements on the ground, either in the countries where they are located or in the targets of their interventions.

We will return later to this aspect of international (Western) feminism in other contexts. Meanwhile, the next chapter outlines in more detail an argument we have encountered in this book already: that feminism must, in fact, acknowledge that 'gender' does not always and in all circumstances, have priority over all other identities.

FEMINISTS AND 'WOMEN'

*'The language that feminism speaks is,
in our experience, also one of dominance
which we have been struggling against.'*

IS FEMINISM ONLY ABOUT 'WOMEN'?

We have seen that feminism is not, in fact, about 'women' but about recognizing how modern discourses of *gender* produce human beings as exclusively 'men' *or* 'women'. We have also seen that feminism is not even about gender alone, but about understanding how gender is complicated by class (as in the case of domestic servants); by caste and by queer politics (as in the case of gay men, *hijras* and intersex identities). In other words, feminism requires us to recognize that 'women' is neither a stable nor a homogeneous category. This question of the entanglement of 'gender' with other identities arises in a variety of contexts globally, and we will consider some of these in what follows.

Let's begin with a crucial identity that complicates gender—religious identity.

INDIA: FROM 'UNIFORM' TO A 'GENDER-JUST' CIVIL CODE

In India, in 1985, Shah Bano became a symbol to be invoked perpetually by organizations of the Hindu Right (especially the Bharatiya Janata Party, the BJP) to establish their 'true' secular credentials and commitment to women's rights as opposed to the 'pseudo-secularists'. Shah Bano was a Muslim woman who claimed maintenance from her divorced husband, in the Supreme Court, under Section 125 of the Criminal Procedure Code, which applies to all citizens of India. Her husband claimed that under the *shariat* or Muslim personal law, it was not necessary for the husband to pay maintenance beyond three months after the divorce. The judgment held that there was no inconsistency between the shariat and Section 125, and granted maintenance to Shah Bano, arousing strong protest from some leaders of the Muslim community, who held this judgment to contravene Muslim personal law. However, there was equally vocal support for the judgment from large sections of the Muslim community, including massive public demonstrations by Muslim women. Ignoring the latter voice, the Rajiv Gandhi government passed an ordinance to overrule the judgment, later passed as the Muslim Women (Protection of Rights on Divorce) Act of 1986, removing Muslim women from the right to maintenance under Section 125.

We must remember that, since the early 1980s, the Congress party had started on a path of instrumentally using communal sentiments for political gains. In the late 1980s to early 1990s, then, we see a series of capitulations by this government, to the sectarian interests of one community and then the other, the Muslim Women Act being one such capitulation.

The Shah Bano issue enabled the BJP to press its general argument of 'appeasement of minorities', and to renew its demand for a uniform civil code (UCC). But we also need to understand why the Shah Bano judgment provoked such an outcry from sections of Muslims when, in two earlier judgments (1979 and 1980), the Supreme Court had upheld the right of Muslim women to maintenance under Section 125 and there had been no reaction.

The debate over the UCC arises from the tension in the Constitution that pits the rights of women as individual citizens against the rights of communities that have the right to their personal laws. Since these personal laws cover matters of marriage, inheritance and guardianship of children, and since all personal laws discriminate against women, the women's movement had made the demand for a UCC as long ago as 1937, long before Independence. However, the UCC has rarely surfaced in public discourse as a feminist issue. It has tended invariably to be set up in terms of 'National Integrity' versus 'Cultural Rights of Community'. The argument for the UCC is made in the name of protecting the integrity of the nation, which is seen to be under threat from the plurality of legal systems and from the very existence of difference from the Hindu/ Indian norm; while the UCC is resisted on the grounds of the cultural rights of communities.

Thus, there always circulates in the public domain some version of the argument that, to be truly secular, India needs a UCC. But the question we must ask is, to what extent is the issue of the Uniform Civil Code about 'secularism'? Is it about the relationship between religious communities and the State? Is it not really about gender-injustice—that is, the constitutionally enshrined inequality between men and women? For instance, Christian women in Kerala were governed by the provisions of the 1916 Travancore–Cochin Christian Succession Act, under which a daughter could inherit only one-fourth of the share of the sons in her father's property. It took a landmark legal struggle by Mary Roy, a Syrian Christian woman, to get a ruling from the Supreme Court in 1986 that Christian women of her community were entitled to have an equal share in their father's property. Of course, in order to avail of this right, women have to be prepared to fight legal battles against their brothers, and most choose not to do so.

The fact is that all personal laws on marriage, and inheritance and guardianship of children, discriminate against women in some form or the other; surely, this should make the issue of the Uniform Civil Code visible in a different way? Should it not be debated as 'India cannot claim be truly *gender-just* as long as discriminatory personal laws exist'?

However, only feminists pose the question in this way. Thus, a party that stands unambiguously for a uniform civil code is the Hindu right-wing BJP, for underlying its national integrity argument is the assumption that while Hindus have willingly accepted reform, the 'other' communities continue to cling to diverse and retrogressive laws, refusing to merge into the national mainstream. As we saw earlier, this is one of modern India's biggest myths, for the Hindu Code did not 'reform' so much as codify heterogeneous practices, to the detriment of the majority of women classified as 'Hindu'. Nevertheless, this understanding marks not only Hindu right-wing arguments but is part of judicial common sense more generally. The judgment on Shah Bano for example, having ruled that the shariat and Section 125 *are mutually consistent* and that there is no disparity between them, went on, contradicting itself, to urge a uniform civil code on the grounds that 'it will help the cause of national integration by *removing disparate loyalties* to laws which have conflicting ideologies' (Kumar 1993: 163; emphasis added).

Later judicial pronouncements on the Muslim Personal Law too—an Allahabad High Court judgment on triple talaq[1] in 1994 and a Supreme Court judgment in the Sarla Mudgal case in 1995—made this argument explicitly. For example, the 1995 judgment stated: 'In the Indian Republic, there was to be only one nation—the Indian nation—and no community could claim to remain a separate entity on the basis of religion' (Agnes 1994).[2]

By the mid-80s, the growing presence of organized Hindutva politics and a general legitimacy for it was becoming evident. The Shah Bano judgment, too, was hailed by the media as a victory against Islamic obscurantism. These developments explain the knee-jerk reaction of the self-styled leadership of the Muslim community to the judgment. Shah Bano herself came under so much pressure from her community that she asked the Supreme Court to record that she now stood against the petition on which it had ruled in her favour, and gave up the maintenance the Court had approved for her.

Shah Bano's own trajectory, the Supreme Court judgment and the subsequent legislation overturning the judgment, all mark the beginning of rethinking by the women's movement on the UCC, which was now revealed in its implicit anti-minority cast and its legitimizing of the national integrity argument. It was increasingly becoming clear to the women's movement that 'national integrity' meant the marginalization of all non-dominant identities and interests.

This disavowal of uniformity by the women's movement in the 1990s is significant in that it marks the recognition of the need to rethink the nation and religious communities as homogeneous entities. Each religious community is a heterogeneous one, and 'Hindu', 'Muslim' and 'Christian' practices differ widely from region to region of India, from sect to sect. Some of these practices are better than others for women, and making them all uniform is *not* a solution to gender-based injustice. It is not even a viable option—what is the uniform standard that will be adopted? The attempt to bring about uniformity has never worked well for women. The following of heterogeneous practices need not be inherently inegalitarian, nor the imposition of a uniform law necessarily the opposite.

For the women's movement then, the focus now is on gender-just laws. The women's movement has since then adopted two strategies: a) bringing about legislation on aspects not covered by personal laws at all, like the Domestic Violence Act (2005) that protects women's rights to the matrimonial home; or certain amendments to the Juvenile Justice Act in 2006 that have now enabled people of all communities to adopt children; and b) supporting initiatives *within* communities to bring about reform.

When reform is initiated 'top-down' by the State in the overall atmosphere of anti-minority politics that India sees today, the fear of minority communities is that reform of personal laws is only a pretext for eroding their identity. However, on-going reform initiatives from inside the communities themselves have a better chance of succeeding. It is not a paradox that some Islamic states (such as Bangladesh) have managed to reform Islamic laws in order to benefit women. When a minority community is threatened with annihilation by majoritarian politics, the obvious response is to close ranks. Only when a community is confident can it afford to be self-critical. Obviously therefore, the Hindu minority in Bangladesh is in a similar position to the Muslim minority in India, despite India's formally proclaimed secularism. When the most vociferous proponents of a uniform civil code are the likes of Narendra Modi, who personally presided over the massacre of Muslims in Gujarat, it does not take much political acumen to realize that it is not women's rights that are on the agenda.

The UCC debate is exemplary from the point of view of understanding the way in which 'uniformity' can work in a democratic polity like India. By emphasizing 'equal' and 'similar' treatment of all communities, the BJP is able to use some aspects of liberal democratic thinking to suggest that any recognition of difference is necessarily contrary to the principles of secularism. Since 'Hindu' has already been equated with 'Indian', Hindu practices by definition can never be merely one of many different practices in India. All 'difference' to be eliminated is thus, necessarily, that of the 'Other' to Hinduism.

Feminists point out that the term 'uniform civil code' has become synonymous in the public mind with reform of what are understood to be barbaric Islamic customs. The judiciary, too, consistently raises the demand for a UCC only in the context of cases dealing with the Muslim Personal Law, never when dealing with cases of gender discrimination in the Hindu Law.

For instance, when a destitute Hindu woman approaches a court for the meagre maintenance permitted under Section

125, Criminal Procedure Code, it is a common ploy for the husband to deny the validity of the marriage by pleading that he has an earlier legal marriage existing and hence, the woman, not being his wife, is not entitled to maintenance. Such an argument is easier to make ever since the Hindu Marriage Act, as we saw earlier, made only one form of the marriage ceremony legal. Thus, a woman may be under the impression she is legally married to a bigamous man, but if he has not followed the *saptapadi* he can claim in court that he is not married to her. What follows is that despite the fact that the man has flouted the law of monogamy as laid down by the Hindu Marriage Act, the woman ends up being denied the crucial and basic right to maintenance.

There have been some judgments in the past that have avoided this; for instance, in 1976, Justice Kania of the Bombay High Court (who later became the Chief Justice of India) had upheld the right to maintenance of a woman in a bigamous marriage. However, a recent ruling by the Supreme Court seems to have undone the positive impact of the earlier judgment. In D. Velusamy vs D. Patchaiammal in 2010, maintenance was denied to women in marriage-like relationships with men who were already married. In this ruling, Justice Markandeya Katju termed such women 'mistresses' and 'keeps' undeserving of maintenance, without a word of reprimand to men in such situations who have duped both the wife and the second woman.[3] However, a later Supreme Court judgment (with Justices H.S. Bedi and Gyan Sudha Mishra on the Bench), declared in August 2011 that a deserted second wife is entitled to maintenance from her husband, regardless of the validity of the marriage. It is not impossible that this judgment was affected by preceding feminist campaigns and indeed, it is desirable that legal opinion should be influenced by changing social attitudes brought about by progressive movements.

This discussion on the transformation of the Uniform Civil Code debate within the women's movement demonstrates the feminist recognition that 'women' do not exist as a single homogeneous category. Was Shah Bano a 'woman' or a 'Muslim'? Thus, even an apparently obvious feminist issue, such as gender-discriminatory personal laws, must be placed within other contexts to be understood in all its complexity.

THE VEIL AND THE MINISKIRT

The projection of Islam as uniquely regressive with regard to women is not unique to India. In Europe, over the past few years, the headscarf or the different forms of veil used by Muslim women has become the emotive symbol by which the West can assert its modernity, the freedom available to its citizens and its belief in gender equality. The recent bans on face-covering veils in European countries are being presented as merely the expansion of older laws that, for security reasons, prohibit people from wearing face-covering items such as masks in public, but the real target is obvious—Islam as linked to both 'terrorism' and to 'oppression of women'.

In Switzerland, a young female basketball player was asked by a regional sports association to stop wearing a headscarf or stop competing. The association cited International Basketball Federation (FIBA) rules that ban all religious symbols during official games. But as the player Sura Al-

Shawk pointed out, many players have Christian tattoos and wear crosses. FIBA in addition, claimed the headscarf was an 'accessory' that increased the possibility of injury while playing![4] This controversy was indicative of the general mood in Switzerland, for it arose a few months before the nationwide vote in November 2009 that endorsed a ban on minarets, a clearly anti-democratic and anti-Muslim move.

If it is individual freedom that is at stake, then European countries should be ensuring that Muslim women who are forced to wear the veil by their families have access to secular laws that can protect them. But laws banning the headscarf or the veil, rather than empowering Muslim women, in fact attack the freedom of those Muslim women who choose to wear it as an integral part of their religious observance. I see these attempts by European governments to selectively *restrict religious observance* as being exactly parallel to and on par with attempts by Islamic groups to *impose the veil* on Muslim societies in which the veil did not exist, as in Kashmir or Palestine, for example. In both cases, patriarchal power is being directed towards shaping women's identity and behaviour, using them instrumentally as a means towards ends that marginalize them.

Of course, there is also fierce internal resistance from Muslim women and men to Islamic forces imposing specific readings of Islam and of the Quran, but their resistance is weakened—not strengthened—by Western governments restricting freedom of religion for Muslims. For instance, the Revolutionary Association of the Women of Afghanistan (RAWA) had, for decades, struggled against the Taliban, with no support or recognition from anywhere. Suddenly, when the US launched its 'war on terror', RAWA became the staple of CNN broadcasts. At the time, representatives of RAWA repeatedly emphasized that they opposed the American bombing of Afghanistan, seeing it as part of the strategic agenda of the US government and not of the struggle that RAWA had long conducted. They also pointed out that the Northern Alliance whom the US backed, was no less oppressive and patriarchal than the Taliban. Nevertheless, they were appropriated into the battle as allies of the US in the war on terror and used to legitimize US state policy.

In India, too, there are internal voices in the Muslim community that raise objections to religious patriarchies. For instance, the fatwas of Darul Uloom Deoband and other patriarchal seminaries against freedom for women are attacked publicly by Zakia Soman who says she is Muslim and a feminist. 'We work under the framework of Islamic principles and the Indian Constitution,' declares Soman, one of the founding members of Bharatiya Muslim Mahila Andolan (Wajihuddin 2011).

But every Hindu right-wing attack on minorities, every attempt to push through a uniform civil code, makes Soman's task all the more difficult.

So much for the veil. What about the miniskirt, that symbol of liberation? The point that many feminists, including western feminists, disturbed by the bans, have noted, is that the 'freedom' to dress in revealing clothes is equally located within a sexist culture—one ruled by the market—for only a particular kind of body is permitted to be revealed—young, toned, properly depilated, wearing the current style.

Says Naomi Wolf (2008):

> When you choose your own miniskirt and halter top—in a
> Western culture in which women are not so free to age, to
> be respected as mothers, workers or spiritual beings, and to
> disregard Madison Avenue—it's worth thinking in a more
> nuanced way about what female freedom really means.

It is important to recognize that the feminist critique is of
the cultural pressure to dress in particular ways, whether
this involves showing more skin or covering up. In either
case, the element of force is what we isolate as the problem,
not the dress itself. For instance, in 2011, the Badminton
World Federation (BWF) announced its new dress code
requiring women players to wear skirts 'to ensure attractive
presentation of badminton.' Of course, most workplaces
have dress codes. But the problem here is the blatant sexism
of this requirement, for what the BWF was saying quite
openly was that they expected more people to come to the
sport if they could expect to see suggestively flying skirts
(on women). There were protests from all the top women
players of India on grounds of comfort while playing and
personal preference. Chinese players, too, raised objections
(Beijing Olympics doubles winner Yu Yang: 'I don't like
wearing skirts. I am not used to them. When I wear a skirt,
I don't know how to play'). Two-time mixed doubles world
champion Indonesian Lilyana Natsir said: 'Skirts hamper my
movement when I play' (Menon 2011). As Eliza Truitt put it
in an article on tennis gear, if skirts were more comfortable
or conducive to better play, male tennis players looking for

a competitive edge would have adopted skirts long ago, just as male athletes shave their legs and don body stockings for swimming (Truitt 2001).

Religious objections predictably made their appearance. Badminton Asia Confederation Vice-President Syed Naqi Mohsin said that the rule would be discriminatory. Not to 'women', as feminists might feel, but to 'Muslims'. 'The BWF states that the new regulation will not discriminate against any religion or beliefs. How can wearing skirts not clash with the religious beliefs of female Muslim players?' (Menon 2011)

Eventually the BWF backed off, but what was interesting was the foregrounding of 'religious' and 'Muslim' objections by the media, over the completely non-religious and profession-related objections made by the women players. One wonders whether, if 'Muslim' objections had not kicked in, the opinion of women players would have counted for much!

We move now to another identity-complicating gender that is quintessentially Indian—caste.

CASTE AND WOMEN

The growing visibility and the militancy of caste politics during the 1990s have increasingly forced the recognition that 'woman' is not simply an already existing subject that the women's movement can mobilize for its politics. This is most clearly revealed by the debate that has been underway since the late 1990s around reservations for women in Parliament. The Women's Reservation Bill (WRB) that proposes to reserve 33 per cent of seats in Parliament for women has been pending for well over a decade, and what is holding it up is assumed to be the opposition of patriarchal forces.

But while the proponents of the measure base their claims on the idea of gender justice, the opposition to the proposed legislation cannot simply be categorized as patriarchal, for it comes from a particular caste location that includes women, which expresses the legitimate apprehension that a blanket reservation of 33 per cent for women (the current proposal being debated), would simply replace 'lower'-caste men with 'upper'-caste women. The democratic upsurges of the 1980s transformed Parliament from a largely upper-class and upper-caste, English-educated body to one that more closely resembles the mass of the population of India in terms of class, caste and educational background. Today, an immediate conversion of one-third of the existing seats into reserved seats for women is likely to bring into the fray largely those women who already have the cultural and political capital to contest elections and, in an extremely unequal society like India, these are bound to be élite women.

Thus, the argument against the current form of the Bill is a claim that reservations for women should take into account other disempowered identities among women—that is, the 'quotas within quotas' position, which says that there should be a further reservation within the 33 per cent, for OBC (Other Backward Classes)[5] and Muslim women. (The 22.7 per cent reservation for SC/ST women is a constitutional requirement that would come into operation automatically.)

In other words, the sharp opposition to the Bill cannot simply be dismissed as anti-women. Take, for instance, the notorious comment by the OBC leader of Janata Dal

(United) party, Sharad Yadav, who claimed that Parliament would be overrun by 'short-haired women' (*par-kati mahilaen*). This statement has been widely attacked for its misogyny, but we do need to see it as expressing a legitimate fear that the composition of Parliament would be radically altered overnight, in favour of upper classes and upper castes. The image of women with stylish short hair draws upon a common stereotype of Westernized and élite women. Now, of course this is a stereotype, but it also reflects a social reality. Surely we are not under the impression that all the support for women's reservation comes from strongly anti-patriarchal sources. These are the very parties which consistently refuse to field women candidates, and which have hardly any women in decision-making positions unless they have the right kind of family tree. It is the patriarchal operation of these very parties—from CPI(M) to BJP (and all the others in between)—for sixty-five years that has made reservations for women necessary in the first place.

So, is the fear justified that the WRB is an upper-caste ploy to stem the tide of lower-caste men in Parliament? Let us look at the experience of reservations for women at the local level, in Panchayati Raj Institutions (PRI), since 1992. Studies in several states (for instance, Gujarat, Karnataka, and West Bengal) have confirmed that while there has been a positive impact on the lives of the elected women themselves, by and large, reservations for women have strengthened the entrenched power of the dominant caste groups of the area. That is, men of less dominant castes in PRI have been replaced by women of the dominant castes (Menon 2004). Unsurprisingly, it seems that a blanket reservation for 'women' brings to power women of dominant groups and castes in society. An immediate filling of 33 per cent seats with a supposedly undifferentiated category of 'women' would certainly change the caste character of Parliament in the short term at least, to one more comfortable to many. How else can one understand BJP's determined opposition to the Mandal Commission reservations for OBCs and its equally fervent support for women's reservations? Counterpose (upper-caste) women against OBC (men)— that appears to be the winning formula.

What I fail to understand is why the 'quotas within quotas' position is so unacceptable to those supporting the WRB. After all, surely the idea of reservations for women in Parliament is not based on the understanding that the biological category called women needs to be represented? If we are arguing that the social experience of being positioned as women within the current economic, cultural and political arrangements is disadvantageous vis-à-vis men, and needs to be reflected in Parliament, then we need to accept that this experience is inflected differently by caste and community— that is, the social experience of being an upper-caste, urban Hindu woman, while definitely shaped by one kind of patriarchy, is nevertheless different from the experience of being an OBC or Muslim woman. Why shouldn't the latter also have representation in Parliament? So the opposition to the proposal (an acceptance of which could lead to the end of an impasse that has lasted for over a decade) by those who wish to see the legislation passed, can only be understood as discomfort with precisely the entry of these caste groups into Parliament.

It may be noted that the opposition to the legislation in India is not that the category of citizen is universal and should remain 'unmarked' by any other identity, that its universalism should not be fractured by introducing gender identity. Rather, the opposition to it is in the form of insisting that more identities and differences (caste/community) should be inserted into that of gender—the 'quotas within quotas' position. Here, a comparison to a similar move in France is instructive.

The parity movement in France, which emerged in the 1990s, was a demand for complete equality, that is, numerically equal representation for women and men in decision-making bodies, especially elected assemblies. However, the debates over the issue played out very differently in France than in India. In France, the recognition of gender in citizenship was seen as antithetical to democracy, to universal citizenship in which no difference should be recognized; while those who defended parity too, claimed the universal position—that citizenship would be more truly universal only when gender was recognized. Thus, all arguments there on the issue of parity—both feminist pro- and anti-parity positions as well as anti-feminist denunciations of parity—were largely in terms of different kinds of reassertion of the universal.

It is clear that the distinctive historical trajectories of the two democracies have created different sets of concerns about citizenship and representation—France having undergone a 'classic' bourgeois democratic revolution in the eighteenth century, and India becoming a postcolonial democracy two hundred years later, where the ideal of the abstract and the individual citizen as the basis for democracy was never unambiguously enshrined as it was in the European context. Thus, feminist politics must always be sensitive to the significance of different locations—different in terms of both the time period and the geographical location (Menon 2004).

The challenges to feminist politics from caste politics also erupt in the context of 'upper'-caste feminists addressing patriarchy within Dalit communities. For instance, S. Anandhi suggested, in a study of a Tamil village, that competing performances of masculinity by Dalit and upper-caste men in the context of rapid socio-economic transformation, place a disproportionate burden on women, both Dalit and non-Dalit. The empowerment of male Dalit youths—due to the opening up of non-agricultural avenues of income—it was argued, is marked by hyper-masculinity, which is most often asserted against women—their 'own' as well as those of the 'other'. In a critical response, C. Lakshmanan argued that the study and the very use of the 'imported' category of masculinity 'reinforces hegemonic stereotypes of the newly empowered aggressive, macho heterosexual male', who can only be 'a violator of the female self', thus posing men and women as groups in perpetual contradiction to each other. His critique suggested that Dalit men and women had shared interests in opposition to non-Dalit men and women. He characterised the study as a manifestation of discomfort with growing Dalit assertion, by Brahmin as well as non-Brahmin/Dravidian feminists[6] (Anandhi et al. 2002; Lakshmanan 2004).

Another revealing moment of tension was manifested at the seventh National Conference of Autonomous Women's

Movements in Kolkata (2006), between the newly politicized bar-dancers of Mumbai (about whom we will learn more later) and the Dalit feminist groups, who found it impossible to support bar-dancing as a profession. Dalit feminists argued that such forms of 'entertainment' were not only patriarchal, but also casteist, since many Dalit women come from castes that are traditionally forced into such professions. Thus, the discomfort of Dalit feminists with sex work and professions (such as dancing for male audiences in bars), which are seen to be related to prostitution, cannot be seen only in terms of conventional morality. There are sharply political and equally feminist positions ranged on both sides, and the opposition between them is not easily amenable to an élite/ subaltern division since both identities, as in this case (Dalit and bar-dancer), are often equally subaltern.

Among Dalit women, there is a general suspicion of mainstream Indian feminism: they see it as being dominated by privileged, dominant caste and upper-class, urban feminists and their issues. Dalit intellectual Cynthia Stephen came up with the term 'Dalit Womanism' to describe a different politics. The inspiration was from Black women in the US who coined a new term 'Womanism' to describe their vantage point, from which they saw Black men less as patriarchal oppressors and more as comrades in their struggle against racism, which white feminists were as responsible for perpetrating as white men.

Stephen (2009) writes:

And with a visceral rejection of the oxymoronic term Dalit Feminism I feel the best way to go for us is to call our struggle Dalit Womanism, and to acknowledge that the language that feminism speaks is, in our experience, also one of dominance which we have been struggling against.

At the same time, it is important to note that mainstream feminist scholarship and politics today struggles with its own legacy of exclusion of caste, and there are explosive engagements between 'Dalit' and 'Savarna' feminists, which I am optimistic enough to consider productive for both.[7]

'WOMEN AND PEACE'

The French Nobel Prize winning writer Romain Rolland said, 'Where order is injustice, disorder is the beginning of justice.'

Peace and order are not necessarily just. Often, peace and order rest on a dominant order that maintains itself through a combination of force and hegemony.* Coercion is exercised and hegemony produced through institutions ranging from army and police to schools, the family and religious institutions; often, both involve the law, which predominantly maintains an order that is in the interest of propertied and dominant groups.

There is disorder and conflict all over the world—movements for national self-determination, struggles against land acquisition by the State, against the dispossession of indigenous people. In such a scenario, where you find different kinds of resistance to the project of the nation state, to capitalism, to the project of unjust social order, what does it mean to talk of 'conflict resolution' and 'peace'? You

---

* That policeman inside your head who tells you how to behave.

cannot resolve a conflict unless you remove the inequality and the injustice that underlie it. It is not a matter of getting opposing sides to sit and talk to each other—if one party is very powerful and the other is completely powerless, the conflict can be resolved only in one way. So, sometimes conflicts should not be 'resolved', but should lead to the destabilization of the old order and the establishment of a new, more just social order.

Behind the notion of a special role for women in peace and conflict resolution lies the assumption that across all other identities, 'women' have a common bond—women are mothers, women are nurturing, women want peace. But women can be combatants, they can be violent; they can also want peace, they can want to resolve conflict; just like men, they too can have a range of motivations.

Of course, it is possible in certain kinds of contexts for women to use their conventional identity to be peace activists in quite creative ways. So, for example in Sri Lanka, the political formation called The Mothers' Front that emerged between 1990 and 1993, had a huge grass-roots membership. Basically, these activists were mothers protesting the disappearance of their sons and male relatives. In many conflict situations, including the north-east of India, Kashmir and Sri Lanka, 'disappearance' has a particular meaning. Young men—and mostly they are men—vanish, usually taken away by the State and sometimes by militants. For three years, the Mothers' Front actively used their identity as mothers: on the one hand, presenting themselves in traditional ways as mothers who care, emphasizing their maternal suffering; and on the other hand, presenting these sentiments politically, in the public arena. Malathi de Alwis suggests that in this way, they continuously subverted the idea of motherhood—which is seen as a private and individual identity—because although they invoked maternal suffering, they were not sitting at home and suffering, they were marching militantly on the streets, confronting the Sri Lankan State (de Alwis 1997). The 'Women in Black' in Latin America and many others too, have politically used and creatively played with this identity of motherhood.

In the US today, there is a kind of subversive maternalist politics in which militant feminists have been fighting for better working conditions for women, better childcare facilities, maternity and paternity leave, and so on. But there can also be a conservative maternalistic politics where motherhood and the special moral responsibility of mothers are used to defend the dominant status quo with all its social inequalities intact. So maternalism is not always radical or progressive, it can lead to a very conservative politics.

This is why 'women and peace' initiatives in conflict zones all over the world, where militant movements are in confrontation with armed forces of the State, often face criticism from women within these movements. The invocation of 'peace' and the unproblematic assumption that 'women' are necessarily committed to it rather than to 'conflict', such critics argue, is in effect an attempt to break the solidarity of the embattled community through the supposed unity of 'women'. For such critics, the active presence of women in armed organizations and their commitment to the goals of those struggles illustrates their greater solidarity with the men of their community than with the women of the oppressor community.

*

'Woman' then, is not a natural and self-evident identity, the obvious subject of feminist politics. The subject of feminist politics has to be brought into being by political practice. There are no pre-existing 'women' who may be Hindu or Muslim, upper-caste or Dalit, white or black; rather, there are 'people' who may respond to different kinds of political challenges, as 'Dalit' or 'Muslim' or as 'women'. The success of feminism lies precisely in its capacity to motivate 'people' to affirm themselves *as* feminists in different kinds of contexts.

But equally importantly, sometimes, a feminist will have to recognize that the defining factor at work in a particular situation may be race or caste, not gender; just as conversely, a Dalit activist or a Marxist will have to recognize the defining feature in some situation as gender, not caste or class. All radical political activists and theorists then, necessarily also must be feminists.

VICTIMS OR AGENTS?

'Nothing can be more universal or elementary than the fact that choices of all kinds in every area are always made within particular limits'

As must have become clear by now, there are as many disagreements among feminists as there are solidarities, hence, the emergence of the term 'feminisms' in the plural. The common ground among feminists is marked by the recognition that gendered power relations oppress women and prevent them from attaining their full potential, but there are sharp differences of opinion regarding the manner in which these power relations operate in specific contexts and how they intersect with other power relations. Some of these disagreements have unfolded over the previous pages.

In this chapter, we explore one of the key debates: When are women to be considered as **victims** needing protection, and when as active **agents** engaging with power and carving out their own spaces? The notion of 'choice' is not enough to answer this question—that if people 'choose' to do something, it reflects their agency. It is not enough because 'freedom of choice' is always exercised within strict boundaries that are non-negotiable—these boundaries are defined by economic class, by race and caste and, of course, by gender. The freedom to choose is never absolute—a domestic servant's child cannot simply choose to be a doctor, a woman cannot simply choose her own future unconditionally. And yet, within those limited boundaries, people do make choices. How are we, as feminists, to understand these choices?

As Amartya Sen (2006) puts it:

> [N]othing can be more elementary and universal than the
> fact that choices of all kinds in every area are always made
> within particular limits. For example, when we decide what
> to buy at the market, we can hardly ignore the fact that
> there are limits on how much we can spend. The 'budget
> constraint,' as economists call it, is omnipresent. The fact
> that every buyer has to make choices does not indicate
> that there is no budget constraint, but only that choices
> have to be made within the budget constraint the person
> faces. What is true in elementary economics is also true in
> complex political and social decisions.

We will consider here five different issues in which the agency/
victimhood dilemma has been played out in complicated
ways for feminists. Three of these can be thought of as forms
of sexualized labour: *sex work, bar-dancing* and *commercial
surrogacy*. The other two are *pornography* and *abortion*.
Debates around all these have developed in directions that
seriously trouble settled feminist critiques of violence,
sexuality and above all, 'choice'.

But first, a discussion of a term commonly used by
feminists, 'commodification', which runs through many of
these debates.

COMMODIFICATION

The term 'commodification of the female body' refers to
a form of critique that feminists have long made, of certain

kinds of representation of female bodies—as objects of male desire, as saleable in the market. From the scantily-clad, sexualized bodies of women in advertisements for luxury items that assume a male consumer, to highly-commercialized beauty contests, to women who 'sell their bodies', that is, give sex in exchange for money—all these have come within the framework of commodification. Derived from Marx, the term is often loosely used to suggest the pollution—by market values—of objects and relationships that should properly be outside of commerce.

But in a world in which everyone makes a living, or tries to make a living, by selling a faculty (intellect, musical ability, training of various kinds, physical labour) or an object (from agricultural produce to mobile phones to cheap and shiny objects at traffic lights), this kind of critique has lost its edge. Is a professor commodifying her mind when she accepts payment for teaching? And if so, why is this acceptable to feminists and not, say, a woman commodifying her body parts to advertisers, or to clients who have sex with her? One answer would be to say that the former has greater dignity and social respect than the latter but, as feminists, we should question the ways in which 'dignity' and 'social respect' are assigned to some forms of work and not to others? To intellectual labour, but not to manual labour? Surely the feminist task is to upturn these values, to transform the ways in which we look at the world, and not to reaffirm the world as it is?

Perhaps we should go back and take a closer look at what Marx said about commodification, and see whether that helps in any way to rethink these paradoxes. Marx used the term 'commodity' to refer to something that has exchange value, a thing that can be bought and sold in the market. A commodity appears to be a 'mysterious' thing, said Marx, because the human labour that has gone into its production is obscured, and the commodity appears to be a purely physical object with a value that is *intrinsic* to it. Human labour is performed in a network of social relations, but this fact is hidden, and commodities appear to relate directly to one another. Take, for instance, the comparative value of iron and gold, which appears to be the result of the intrinsic nature of those minerals when, in fact, their value is determined by the socially established conventions of exchange that establish gold as 'more precious' than iron. And of course, these assigned values totally ignore the human labour involved in transforming iron and gold into commodities, from their initial form as naturally occurring minerals.[1]

It is this critique of the commodity form under capitalism that has been extended by feminism to the ways in which the female body is produced as a commodity. But as the discussion above suggests, the application of this critique to human bodies is to lose sight of human agency, will, volition, or whatever one may term the fact that human beings think and make choices, while the objects produced by them do not.

Now, Marx also says about the commodity:

> It is plain that commodities cannot go to market and make exchanges on their own account. We must therefore have recourse to their guardians, who are also their owners . . . In order that these objects may enter into relations with each other as commodities, their guardians must place themselves in relation to one another.[2]

This mutual recognition by guardians of one another as owning their commodities is established in capitalist society through the contract.

This idea of the contract involves the myth of two equal individual parties mutually agreeing to certain terms and conditions of exchange—of labour or commodities—for money. Marx himself has, of course, a critique of this myth, for the person selling his/her labour power is not equal in any real sense to the person who employs him/her. The equality is purely formal and legal. But as long as, and to the extent that, work is enabled under capitalist conditions, the idea of the contract is what makes possible a struggle for equitable conditions. After all, why is it preferable to be wage labour than bonded labour? Because at least theoretically, the contract assumes consent and mutually negotiated conditions of work. And at least theoretically, these are protected by law. What, after all, is the Right to Work? A demand to be brought under the capitalist contract.

This is where we come to the problem of extending the critique of commodification to women's bodies. To think of advertising, pornography or sex work as commodification is to think of the women participating in this work as 'commodities', that is, as objects owned by others, men, who are the real parties to the contract. But it is after all women themselves who are parties to the contract. Are they exploited? Yes, of course. But all work under capitalism is 'exploitation', that is, it involves the extraction of surplus value from labour. Under capitalism, the 'choice' that the labour market offers is between more and less arduous, more and less meagrely paid work.

If women choose then, to take up professions like modelling, or sex work, or any other profession in which they commodify some body parts rather than others, should feminists not stand by them in demanding better conditions of work, more pay and dignity in their professions, rather than going along with misogynist values that demean certain kinds of work altogether?

We will see how complicated these internal feminist debates are as we move on to the specific issues.

SEX WORK

Feminism has for long seen prostitution as violence against women, and many feminists still do. However, a new understanding of the practice has emerged with the gradual politicization of people who engage in prostitution, and with their voice becoming increasingly public. One of the key transformations that has come about because of this, is the emergence of the term sex work to replace 'prostitution'.

The understanding behind this is that we need to demystify 'sex'—it is only the mystification of sex by both patriarchal discourses and feminists that makes sex work appear to be 'a fate worse than death'. Consider the preliminary findings of the first pan-India survey of sex workers that we referred to earlier. 3000 women from 14 states and 1 Union Territory were surveyed, all of them from outside collectivized or organized—therefore politically active—spaces, precisely 'in order to bring forth the voices of a hitherto silent section of sex workers.' The significant finding is this: about 71 per cent of them said they had entered the profession willingly.

This study establishes what feminist research on sex work has been increasingly tending to show, that the model of *choice* versus *force* is utterly inadequate in understanding the motivations of women in sex work (Shah 2003). In fact, most sex workers have 'multiple work identities'. The study found that 'a significant number of females move quite fluidly between other occupations and sex work. For example, a street vendor may search for customers while selling vegetables and a dancer at marriages may also take clients. It is not easy to demarcate women's work into neatly segregated compartments. Sex work and other work come together in ways that challenge the differentiation of sex work as an unusual and isolated activity.'

Poverty and limited education are conditions that push women into labour markets at an early age, and sex work was found to be one among several options available to women in the labour market. This means that other occupations are often pursued before sex work emerges or is considered as an option. Sex work offers a significant supplementary income to other forms of labour. Many of those surveyed also worked in diverse occupations in the unskilled manufacturing or services sector for extremely poor wages.

Why did women either leave those other occupations or supplement their income from those occupations with sex work? The responses were:

- low pay
- insufficient salary
- no profit in business
- no regular work

- no seasonal work
- not getting money even after work
- could not run their home with that income—*is kaam se pet nahi bharta*

Quite simply, sex work is an economically attractive option. In short:

> Sex work is not the only site of poor working conditions, nor is it particularly prominent in terms of the employment of minors as compared to other sectors. For those coming to sex work from the other labour markets, they have often experienced equally harsh (or worse) conditions of highly labour intensive work for very low (and most often lower) incomes. It is from these background cases that the significance of sex work as a site of higher incomes or livelihoods emerges (Sahni and Shankar 2011).

What this study does is force us to recognize that 'choice' is severely limited in the labour market as a whole. If people find it possible to move to work that is less exhausting and better paying, they will do so. There is no more or less agency exercised in 'choosing' to work as a domestic servant in multiple households for a pittance and with minimum dignity, or to be exploited by contractors in arduous construction work, than there is in 'choosing' to do sex work—whether as the sole occupation or alongside other work.

We must recognize, when it comes to the capitalist labour market in particular, that 'choice' quite simply does not exist for the vast masses of people. We do recognize this when it comes to other kinds of work—demeaning work, like domestic labour, or exhausting and exploited conditions of work in factories; that is, we see that people do this work only because they have no other choice, but our reaction would not be to demand abolition of that form of work. Rather, we would want the conditions of all kinds of work to be dignified, we would want there to be minimum wage regulations, reasonable leisure time, and so on.

Under prevailing conditions, workers may even be prepared for more arduous hours if it meant a slightly higher wage; that is, they may 'choose' this option. For instance, the Karnataka government decided in early 2011 to amend the Factories Act 1948 to increase the daily working hours of employees from nine to ten hours in an attempt to increase productivity. It claimed that the move was meant to help women workers in the garment industry, and that in fact, the workers themselves had demanded the increase in working hours. Of course, what the workers wanted was an increase in wages, a demand they knew would not have been granted unconditionally. What this 'demand' from the workers showed was that they are grossly underpaid, and so desperate to earn a little more money that they are prepared to work extra (Hunasavadi 2011).

Here you can see the operation of choice—limited but still, exercised within possible limits. The 'choice' to do sex work is no more or less constrained than the choice of any other work is under capitalism. As for forced sex work, which is precisely like bonded labour, as feminists, we should back policies and institutions that support women who want to leave the profession. Then there is the fact that sex workers often face rape and physical abuse from their clients. Decriminalization of sex work would enable such women to take these matters to the law just like any other raped woman (or person of any gender, for that matter).

For most women, isn't marriage far more of a compulsory institution (and compulsory form of work) than any other? For many women it is as arduous, undignified, and inescapable as sex work is assumed to be—and unpaid on top of it all! But we try to empower women within marriages, not demand the abolition of marriage itself.*

The growing sex workers' movement in India thus provokes us into questioning the assumption that it is better to be one man's wife, effectively subject to feudal power relations, than a sex worker, subject to a capitalist contract. An alternative way in which organized sex workers conceptualize their work is to move away from the idea of being a 'worker', a wage slave under capitalism, to a person running her own business. In many parts of India, prostitution is referred to as *dhanda*, business, and women who engage in prostitution are referred to as *dhandewali*, women in business. The Maharashtra-based sex-worker organizations, SANGRAM and VAMP, prefer this as a self-description as opposed to *jaun karmi* or sex worker, which is used by the Durbar Mahila Samanwaya Committee (DMSC) in West Bengal. Thus the former use the term, 'people in

---

* Although it is worth considering the kinds of imaginative horizons that might open up if marriage were indeed to be abolished. Would it result in children being brought up entirely differently if that compulsory future were not on the horizon, and those compulsory roles did not have to be performed?

prostitution and sex work' (PPS) to acknowledge the diverse groups covered under this term, which include devadasis, housewives who sell sex, women who work in brothels, streetwalkers, and male sex workers. 'Furthermore, the term PPS validates multiple identities by acknowledging people in prostitution and sex work as people first: when she is with a client she is a *dhandewali*; when she is with her children, she is a mother; when she is educating her community, she is a peer educator' (Pillai et al. 2008).

The debate on regulation of sex work falls broadly into three positions:

Criminalization, a view that considers prostitution to be a social evil. This can produce either an actively abolitionist position, or a more hypocritical one that tolerates it by remaining silent on whether the activity itself is legal or not, while criminalizing the 'outward manifestations of sex work', such as, soliciting, brothel-keeping and trafficking. The current Indian legislation—the Immoral Traffic (Prevention) Act of 1986 (called either ITPA or PITA for short)—is an example of the latter approach.

Legalization involves the legalizing and state regulation of sex-work through zoning and licensing laws. The Kolkata-based sex workers' union, Durbar Mahila Samanwaya Committee, has pointed out in a publication that the colonial experience in India has shown that legalization results in excessive state control and ghettoization of sex work. This approach is also criticized for its potential to push large sections of the sex trade underground.

Decriminalization treats sex work as falling within livelihood issues and as a matter between consenting adults and therefore, demands the removal of sex work and all voluntary relationships around it from the scope of criminal law. Under this approach, forced sex work, as well as that involving minors, could be subjected to the force of general laws on fraud, coercion and forced labour, while voluntarily undertaken sex work would come under the scope of existing labour legislation. This is the position generally taken by organized sex workers all over the world, including in India (Kotiswaran 2011).

The complexities of this debate are obscured by pronouncements such as those of the Supreme Court (in 2009) which, while hearing a Public Interest Litigation on child-trafficking, asked the government to legalize prostitution if it was unable to curb it. 'You can then monitor the trade, rehabilitate and provide medical aid to those involved,' said the judges. As we saw though, legalization versus abolition are not the only two positions possible, and there are serious problems that sex workers' movements have with legalization.

BAR-DANCERS

A related issue that women's groups have taken up is that of 'bar-dancers' in Mumbai. Bar-dancers used to perform floor shows and cabarets in licensed bars, and the 1980s saw a proliferation of such bars. Bar dancers were not sex workers but when the state of Maharashtra banned dancing in bars in 2005, the reasons adduced were similar to those usually made for the abolition of prostitution—'depravation of public morality', and 'corruption of youth'. Women's groups from Mumbai and other cities, as well as the labour union of the dancers themselves, came together to protest the move as denying the affected women the right to livelihood. The hypocrisy of the ban becomes clearer when we consider the fact that it applied only to low-end 'bars' and not to 'hotels' frequented by more wealthy clients, as the state proposed an exemption to clubs and to hotels which had three or more 'stars'. Similarly, a Delhi High Court judgment (in 2006) overturned a 1914 law which prohibited women from serving liquor in public places. The judges were ruling on a petition filed by the Hotel Association of India and two women hotel employees, who said the law was damaging their career prospects. The reason the judges gave for upholding their claim reinforces sexualized images of women in the public sphere, namely that '. . . the feminine touch indeed lends grace and elegance to the hospitality industry, which grace and elegance is not inherently suited to the male disposition'. In the bar-dancers' case, the Bombay High Court, in April 2006, ruled as unconstitutional the Maharashtra government ban on dance bars, conceding that it violated the fundamental right to livelihood. The case is now in appeal in the Supreme Court but in the meanwhile, the women have scattered back into the invisibility from which the publicity had dragged them.

The Mumbai-based feminist group, Majlis, that intervened in the case along with the bar-dancers' union, found in the course of its investigations that the dancers were largely migrants from other parts of India, who had been brought to the city with the promise of jobs as domestic labour, but then were introduced to the bars. However, although the women may have been initially apprehensive about the work involved in bar-dancing, most of them eventually found it to be the best option since they were earning far more than they would as domestic workers and they enjoyed a certain degree of economic freedom. Majlis found that 'There was no compulsion, other than their own economic compulsion, that made them become bar-dancers.' The ban, on the contrary, resulted in many of them being jailed, without the wherewithal to get out on bail, leaving their aged parents, children and sometimes, infants in arms to fend for themselves. The closure of the bars led to destitution for many even if they were not in jail (Majlis 2005).

The sheer callousness—of the moral framework that declares sex work and bar-dancing to be intolerable but can, with equanimity, tolerate the poverty and desperation of people thrown out of this work—is mind-boggling.

'TRAFFICKING' (FORCED) VERSUS 'MIGRATION' (VOLUNTARY)— CHALLENGES TO NATIONAL BORDERS

The notion of 'trafficking in persons' has become closely linked to the abolitionist position on sex work, and has acquired great clout and visibility internationally, with feminists from the first world leading anti-trafficking campaigns. The most widely used definition of trafficking within such campaigns was jointly arrived at in 1999 by the Global Alliance Against Traffic in Women (GAATW), the Foundation Against Trafficking in Women, and the

International Human Rights Law Group (IHRLG) based in the US. In this definition, trafficking is linked to migration, with trafficking being understood as 'forced migration.'

Many feminists are critical of anti-trafficking initiatives, particularly of the US Anti-Trafficking Act 2000. They show they these initiatives collapse the distinction between (voluntary) sex work and (coerced) trafficking, treating all cross-border movements of women as coerced, thereby excluding these women from legal recognition and casting their families as criminals. There has been pressure on the US government from international groups working on public health and human rights, to rethink the current US law that makes funds for HIV/AIDS prevention programmes conditional on opposing prostitution. Such a requirement— it is argued by feminist critics of anti-trafficking campaigns— vitiates health programmes among sex workers and fails to protect the most vulnerable sections. There is also militant opposition from sex workers themselves to anti-trafficking policies being promoted by Western and South Asian countries and some feminist and human rights groups (Kapur 2005). Anti-trafficking initiatives are thus another instance of 'governance feminism' that we discussed earlier, and face the same critique.

Feminist legal scholar and activist Flavia Agnes has suggested a conceptual move away from the notion of a *vulnerable subject* to that of a *risk-taking subject*. She argues that migrants and trafficked persons, including those in prostitution, exercise agency and demonstrate decision-making abilities, which seek to maximize their own survival as well as that of their families. For example, many women negotiate the terms of their own movement and utilize technological networks to plan their migration and keep in contact with others in their country of origin. Women's perception of themselves and of their 'exploiters' provides a further challenge to the traditional and stereotypical images of victim and perpetrator. For example, while the dominant image of women in the sex industry is one of subjugated, dominated, objectified and abused persons who are preyed upon by conniving men, studies of women in the sex tourism industry in various countries reveal that women view it as an arena of negotiations to improve their own economic situation.

In addition, Agnes points out, as do many other feminists, that the trafficking agenda has come to be increasingly influenced by a conservative sexual morality which casts 'good' women as modest, chaste and innocent. Challenges to this understanding are seen as posing a dual threat—to women themselves and to the security of society. This produces a 'protectionist agenda', within which no distinction is drawn between willed and coerced movement. All movement of women is seen as coerced, thus reinforcing assumptions of third-world women as victims, infantile and incapable of decision-making (Agnes 2006).

Nandita Sharma has suggested that anti-trafficking campaigns need to be replaced with a political practice that questions the very legitimacy of sealed national borders that we have come to take for granted over the last century. National border regimes must be opened up as well as the labour markets organized through them. There must be an end to discrimination based on one's nationality. These are the demands of the growing group of the No Border Network activists across the world. A radical political practice is called for, that challenges the barbed-wire borders of nation states (Sharma 2003).

Thus we see that opening up the question of 'prostitution' from a variety of feminist perspectives reveals serious fissures in a range of concepts assumed to be stable and unquestionable—from 'nation states' to the idea of the 'work' itself.

COMMERCIAL SURROGACY

Commercial surrogacy, discussed earlier in the context of the family, is another phenomenon that frontally raises the issue of commodification of the woman's body, as well as the question of agency and choice.

The term gestational surrogacy (or surrogate pregnancy) generally refers to a woman carrying to term in her uterus, an embryo implanted through in vitro fertilization (IVF). Commercial gestational surrogacy normally involves the sperm and egg of the contracting party, and a financial transaction in which the contracting party pays the woman who will bear the foetus for them in her uterus.

A complex field of ethical concerns around commercial surrogacy has been outlined by feminists over the last decade or so. In vitro fertilization, as a medical intervention, has long been under the feminist scanner for the tremendous physical and emotional stress it places on women who undergo the process. With commercial surrogacy, a whole new arena of power relations has opened up between relatively powerless surrogates from poorer parts of the globe and wealthy heterosexual, and also homosexual, contracting couples. And veritable cottage industries of commercial surrogacy have sprung up in several parts of the world. Feminists have raised the question of national health priorities: Is infertility really the most important health problem in poor countries? They have also placed the surrogacy debate within the framework of reproductive rights and justice, trying to bring to the fore the rights of the poor women who become surrogates (Qadeer and John 2008; Waldby 2010; Sarojini and Das, 2010).

There is considerable feminist discomfort over conceptualizing a woman's 'natural body' as the object of a contractual relationship. Repugnance towards such objectification is reflected in, for instance, the testimony of American feminist academic and activist Janice Raymond before the House Judiciary Committee of Michigan in 1987, declaring that surrogacy contracts 'should be made unenforceable as a matter of public policy . . . they reinforce the subordination of women by making women into reproductive objects and reproductive commodities.'[3] The very language used in technological and contractual reproduction dehumanizes women, referring to them as 'maternal environments' and 'human incubators'; and by the use of terms such as fishing/recruiting/harvesting of eggs; miscarriages being attributed to an 'incompetent cervix', and so on (Raymond 1993; Sarojini and Das 2010). The surrogates become mere reproductive machines, and are seen as nothing more than the sum of their reproductive parts.

Another kind of feminist response, however, emphasizes the agency of women entering into a surrogacy contract, and, in an argument that parallels feminist debates on sex work, explores the positive implications of treating surrogacy as a form of labour. Amrita Pande suggests that we should think of commercial surrogacy in a poor country such as India, in terms of new forms of 'informal, gendered and stigmatized work', with commercial surrogacy being a form of 'sexualized care work' (2009). Studies of commercial surrogates in Israel and India have found that they have a complex understanding of what they are doing; and different ways of conceptually separating their role as mothers towards the children they bear for themselves, and their relationship to the children they bear for others for money. They are not simply brainwashed and helpless dupes, but women who have made certain choices having thought the circumstances through (Pande 2009; Teman 2003).

Even as women's organizations and feminists are beginning to come to terms with this phenomenon, a draft Assisted Reproductive Technologies (Regulation) Bill is already on the anvil. Feminist analyses of this Bill reveal that the stakeholders are assumed to be two parties only—the contracting parents and the medical practitioners. The surrogate mother is addressed only in terms of the interests of the contracting parents; for instance, she cannot have sex for a year and a half from the beginning of the process until delivery; a married woman requires the permission of her husband. On the other hand, the terms of her compensation and the agent who will compensate her are not clear; there is no anticipation of or remedies considered in the event of her becoming HIV positive in the process. The Bill, in effect, turns most of the surrogate's transactions into a private undertaking with the future parents, with no safeguards built in to protect her interests (Qadeer and John 2008).

One of the reasons for the absence of the voice of surrogates themselves in this debate has to do with the anonymity preferred by most surrogate mothers, because of prevailing social prejudices. But in any case, feminist politics tends to be representational; that is, there is a sense in which 'feminists' assume they know what is in the interests of 'women'. So, if democratic pressure is built up, women's organizations and feminist scholars/activists can become involved in the drafting of the legislation. But unless some sort of community of surrogate mothers themselves comes into being, evolving its own rules, even such a legislation may not protect their interests. A law devised by feminists representing the interests of 'women who become surrogates', whose interests we presume to understand because 'we are all women', can at best be potentially useful but at worst, may make it difficult for women to make an income in this way.

For instance, one feminist intervention in the debate demands an end to anonymity of surrogate mothers because that can leave them in a very vulnerable position. While one understands the feminist impulse behind this demand, how many women are empowered enough to risk their identity being known, given the sexualized understanding of the work? Why should they not have the right to remain anonymous? An insistence on removing anonymity could reduce opportunities for women to take up such work.

When women doing commercial surrogacy organize themselves, and start to voice their experiences, then we will begin to understand dimensions of this work that we are not in a position to at this time.

PORNOGRAPHY

Indian feminism of the 1970s and 1980s targeted sexist films, posters and advertisements by picketing films and physically pulling down offensive hoardings and posters, among other actions. The understanding of 'sexism' and 'offensiveness' here was restricted to the exploitative representation of women's bodies, or the direct glorification of rape. A broader definition of sexism would have brought into the net almost every film ever made by the mainstream Indian film industry, which has portrayed women either as submissive or as punished in the end for their assertiveness; the heroine as the target of aggressive romancing by the hero which stops barely short of sexual harassment, and which she simperingly accepts, and so on. It was hoped that by targeting the most obvious ways in which women's bodies were depicted by the film industry, this broader climate of misogyny and sexism would also be made visible. Lobbying by women's organizations resulted in a new law—The Indecent Representation of Women (Prohibition) Act, 1986, passed with what seemed in retrospect to be great speed and very little debate.

Even at the time, the law was greeted with ambivalence by feminists. In their book on the Indian women's movement, Nandita Gandhi and Nandita Shah, although critical of the powers given to the State, simultaneously felt the law was too full of loopholes—it did not cover advertisements, posters and photographs; did not define 'indecent representation' sufficiently clearly, thereby leaving room for judicial interpretation; and did not specifically mention women and the gendered nature of power relations. In other words, the criticism they had was that the law both gave the State too much power and covered too few areas (Gandhi and Shah 1992).

A new entrant into the campaign against 'obscenity' in the 1990s was the Hindu right-wing. Feminist interventions too, continued in this decade, if at a lower level but a different feminist voice was also emerging, challenging both right-wing and feminist demands for censorship. Three main themes emerged in this debate.

First, on the question of sexuality and desire, the troubling continuity in the pro-censorship positions of the Hindu right-wing and of secular feminists. The former attacks 'obscenity' and promiscuous 'Western' culture as a threat to traditional 'Indian' values, while the feminist argument is as critical of traditional Indian values as it is of sexist representations of women. Nevertheless, pro-censorship feminists unwittingly participate in the Hindu right-wing policing of sexuality and perpetuate the idea that women are not sexual agents themselves, but always the victims of pornography. Many anti-censorship feminists argue that we should be trying to create and protect spaces of greater sexual expression for women. Rather than closing off public spaces to sexuality, we should work towards a proliferation of sexual imagery directed at women's desires.

Second, the issue of the State. The journal *Manushi* had noted at the time of the passing of the Indecent

Representation of Women (Prohibition) Act, the arbitrary powers it gave to the State, and the potential curbs on freedom of expression that it could inaugurate.[4] Media scholar Shohini Ghosh argues that terms like 'reasonable regulations', used by feminists inevitably empower a state that feminists do not otherwise trust to remain within democratic limits. In addition, the explosion of media in the 1990s also led some feminists to lament the retreat of the State which left the field of media open to corporate owners. But Ghosh terms this lament 'absurd', for

> the history of state-owned media is one of gaps and absences. All India Radio, Films Division and Doordarshan have consistently erased dissent and marginalised any speech or representation that has run counter to immediate state interests.

Censorship will, she states unequivocally, 'inevitably silence speech on the margins constituted by social, political and sexual minorities.' A revealing illustration of her argument is the controversy over a Hindi film song, *Choli ke peechhe kya hai* (What's behind the blouse). The song was assailed by Hindu right-wing organizations for being obscene, and for creating conditions for increasing sexual harassment of women. Ghosh points out that there were two versions of the song in the film. One, performed by two women to each other on screen and sung by two female singers, and another, with identical lyrics and music, sung and performed by men. This second version culminates in the heroine's being intimidated and physically assaulted by the male protagonist.

But both the legal petition against the song as well as the protesters chose to ignore this latter version:

> The anxiety regarding 'increasing sexual harassment' notwithstanding, the protesters demanded censorship not of the version that actually depicted violence against women but one that represented sexual agency on their part (Ghosh 1999).

The point here is that censorship empowers the State and targets, not the dominant and powerful trends, but the marginal and counter-dominant ones.

A third issue has to do with the question of reception, that is, how pornographic images are received by the audience. All images and representations are *received* differently in different contexts. The *Choli ke peechhe* song performed by two women, for instance, may have appeared sexy to other women too, not just to men. The gaze of the *viewer* constitutes and reconstitutes the meaning of images.

There has thus been a shift in feminist thinking from Laura Mulvey's conception of the 'male gaze' (1975). Mulvey held that in cinema, women are the passive objects of a gaze assumed to be that of the male heterosexual spectator; the camera's gaze on women is necessarily male; and women too take on the male gaze in looking upon themselves. The idea of the male gaze has been widely used in different contexts in feminist theorizing; for instance, with reference to advertising, it has been argued that women are not just the objects of the male gaze, they are themselves the objects being sold to a male spectatorship. However, since the 1990s, feminists have begun to see the female viewer as imbued with agency, engaging dialectically with the images she sees, and producing new meanings unintended by the author of the image. The gaze is not exclusively male, in other words - there are different kinds of gaze.

What constitutes sexuality, pornography and desire, can thus change radically with contexts of time and place. Here is an intriguing story discussed by Udaya Kumar (1997). It is narrated by C. Kesavan, the Ezhava leader of Kerala, in his autobiography. Ezhavas are a 'Backward Caste' that launched powerful struggles for equality through the nineteenth and twentieth centuries. One of the issues in these struggles was defiance of caste-markers, such as Ezhava women not being allowed to cover their breasts. C. Kesavan's mother-in-law relates to him an incident of her youth. At a time when these movements raged across Kerala, she was given some blouses by her sister-in-law. Caught by her mother while secretly wearing the blouse and admiring herself, she was fiercely chastised both for being 'a slut' as well as for walking around 'in shirts like Muslim women'. Scared of her mother's blows, she hid the blouses way, to be worn at night for her husband's enjoyment, who thought they 'looked good', and who would come very late at night to her, she said, like a divine lover, a Gandharva.

The delight in the blouse then, of both the wearer and the viewer, was produced in complex ways—'sexiness' here was produced by the *covering* of breasts secretly at night, in a cultural context in which bare breasts were ordinary and everyday. And then there was the desire generated by the thrill of transgressing caste hierarchy in the dark of the night, in the very rituals of producing 'sex' through robing and disrobing.

We might also remark upon the fact that for the mother, the sign of inappropriate sexuality was the clothing, not the nudity, of the female body, signifying as it did, rule-breaking of two kinds: sluttishness, as well as the loss of carefully designated difference from the Other, the Muslim woman.

Sexuality and desire are dramatically revealed in this instance to be, not something fixed and easily recognizable, but produced at the interstices of 'public' politics and 'private' conjugality.

How do other kinds of non-normative bodies trouble the stable boundaries of what is sexy and what is not? For instance, Anita Ghai posits an insightful distinction between the 'male gaze' and the 'stare' in the context of the disabled female body:

> If the male gaze makes normal women feel like passive objects, the stare turns the disabled object into a grotesque sight. Disabled women contend not only with how men look at women but also how an entire society stares at disabled people.

So de-sexed is the disabled female body considered to be, says Ghai, that in North Indian Punjabi families, where girls are not allowed to sleep in the same room as their male cousins, disabled girls are under no such prohibitions. The assumption that sexuality and disability are mutually exclusive 'denies that people with deviant bodies experience sexual desires' (Ghai 2002).

It is, in fact, impossible to fix the meaning of sexuality. Imagine a classroom in which, during a boring biology class, a drawing was made on the board, of human male and female reproductive systems. Far from being sexy or pornographic, the sketch would have been deadly dull, and transcribed in a bored way into various notebooks. Once the class is over, and a new bunch of boisterous students enters the room, that very same sketch can become the object of adolescent sniggers and knowing sly glances. Without a single thing being changed on the board, a dull educational picture can suddenly become 'pornographic.'

It would appear then, that different kinds of ideas, values and representations construct a mesh which trap some acts as 'sex'. This mesh is historically and geographically fluid, and sieves the material passing through it in different ways at different times: 'sex' is not a clear and specific physical phenomenon always recognizable as such at all times and in all places.

Such an appreciation of the uncontainable fluidity of sexuality and desire, and of the complexity of representational practices, is what lies behind the recent feminist arguments we have discussed, against censorship of 'obscenity' and 'pornography'.

For many Indian feminists, American feminist Carole Vance's notion of 'pleasure and danger' has been very productive. Vance opposes a particular American feminist understanding of pornography as 'the theory behind the practice of rape', in which women can only and always, be the target of an aggressive male sexuality. This view is associated with Catharine MacKinnon and Andrea Dworkin, who are also behind the most powerful anti-trafficking initiatives in the US, and the inspiration for 'governance feminism' discussed earlier. Vance, on the other hand, uses the notions of pleasure and danger to refer to 'the mix of fear and excitement' that women feel when they approach sexuality; to the fact that women, depending on their personal life journeys, may want to stress safety or adventure at different stages in their lives; it suggests that women's responses to sexuality will be diverse, not singular, and that any feminist programme that seeks uniformity in women's responses is 'dishonest and oppressive' (Vance 1984, 1992).

Rather than assume that pornography only objectifies and commodifies women for the male gaze, what if we were to think of women too, as consumers of pornography; of pornography as arousing not only heterosexual desire but also homoerotic desire; and of pornography not as something fixed and easily recognizable but as diffuse and complex as the sensations it evokes? This way of thinking about pornography opens up liberating ways of thinking about not only female sexuality, but about desire in general.

To take on board these insights is to reconcile with the fact that the only defensible feminist position on pornography is to ensure the proliferation of feminist discourses about sexual pleasure and desire, while also recognizing that what is 'feminist' will itself always be the subject of internal contestation.

ABORTION

One of the most troubling issues for feminists in recent years, embodying a dilemma that is almost irresolvable, has to do with the selective abortion of female foetuses. Although this practice is restricted to India and to some South Asian communities in other parts of the world, its very possibility creates a more fundamental crisis for feminism. This is because feminists generally support the unconditional rights of women to safe and legal abortions. They see this as necessary because pregnancy and child-rearing are, for all practical purposes, the sole responsibility of women. They should, therefore, have the right to choose when and under what circumstances they will bring a child into the world, for they should be able to control what happens to their bodies and to their lives. The right to safe and legal abortion is an essential right of self-determination.

In the West, this right has always been challenged and circumscribed by the Christian right-wing, and feminists there, even today, have to struggle to retain it. Anti-abortion campaigns emphasize that the foetus is a person and that it has an independent right to life and so their campaigns position themselves as 'pro-life', while feminists call themselves 'pro-choice'.

The landmark judgment in the US was Roe vs Wade (1973), which defended the right to abortion as a right of privacy. However, this right is precarious, because many states did not repeal the pre-1973 statutes that criminalized abortion, which could again be in force if Roe vs Wade is reversed. Since there is a powerful anti-abortion lobby in the US, this possibility cannot be ruled out. Many American feminists have been uncomfortable about seeing abortion in terms of the rights of individual women and locating it in the realm of privacy, for it suggests that pregnancy is an individual and private matter. They stress rather, that under conditions of pervasive sexism and patriarchy, decisions about pregnancy are sometimes out of the control of women. Moreover, they would like to see decisions about pregnancy and abortion as set within networks of responsibility rather than within the realm of 'individual' rights. We will return to these questions later.

In the UK, abortion has been legal since 1967, but is continuously challenged, most recently in 1987 by a Private Member's Bill, which resulted in substantial debate, but was defeated. In many other countries, abortion is illegal, or is permissible only to save the life of the woman, or only permissible up to the first trimester.

In India, abortion has been legal since the Medical Termination of Pregnancy (MTP) Act of 1971, which came about not because of feminist concerns, or concern for women, but purely as a method of population control. Abortion is legal up to the second trimester, but it is at the *absolute* discretion of medical opinion. A study of the MTP Act points out that the pregnant woman cannot simply state that it is an unwanted pregnancy. She must provide explanations that fit into the conditions listed in the MTP Act, and it is medical opinion that has the power to decide whether the woman meets with the requirements of the Act. That is, expert medical opinion must certify either that the pregnancy involves a risk to the life of the woman, or would cause grave injury to her physical or mental health, or alternatively, that there is a substantial risk that a seriously handicapped child would be born. The Act does not define 'health', 'substantial risk', 'seriously handicapped', and so on. It is left to the medical practitioner to decide how these terms are to be interpreted, although two explanatory notes indicate that pregnancy in the case of rape (excluding marital rape) and contraceptive failure (in the case of a married woman) may be treated as causing injury to mental health. In fact, even the words 'abortion', 'miscarriage' and 'termination of pregnancy' have not been defined, which leaves the medical opinion on these matters sacrosanct.

Thus, the currently liberal-seeming provisions of the MTP Act could become restrictive without a single word of the text being altered (Jesani and Iyer 1993).

But in general, in India, there has been no consistent and organized opinion against abortion. Far from having to struggle for the right to abortion, feminists have found themselves raising questions about the widespread sanction for abortion rather than contraceptives, especially condoms, as a method of controlling population. This means that the physical cost of population control is borne almost entirely by women. Further, feminists have been critical of governments using incentives and disincentives to influence the decisions of government employees regarding family size, and the imposition of the small family norm even where factors like high infant mortality rates and insecurity of income, make it rational to have large families. In the wake of the National Population Policy 2000, several states have announced population policies that have a strongly punitive and anti-democratic thrust. Clearly then, the legal sanction for abortion does not arise from feminist principles at all, but it exists, nevertheless. (Although I must add that of late there have been some very disturbing advertisements on television that promote the contraceptive pill and the morning-after pill, by contrasting them with abortion presented as the most shameful and terrifying alternative, one that any woman should avoid.)

It is another matter that, despite the MTP Act, the number of unsafe abortions continues to be high, and around 20,000 women die every year due to abortion-related complications, most of which are due to their being performed illegally, that is, by unqualified personnel. Medical facilities and trained personnel are inadequate, especially in rural areas and in addition, there is the widely held belief that abortion is illegal. Legalization has not, in short, been buttressed by safe and humane abortion services.

But since the 1980s, these issues have taken a back seat in the face of rising instances of selective abortion of female foetuses. Indian feminists have successfully campaigned for legislation to restrict sex testing during pregnancy. The Pre-Conception and Pre-Natal Diagnostic Techniques (PCPNDT) Act came into effect in 1994, but the sex ratio at birth has continued to fall, showing that sex-selective abortion continues unchecked.

The problem is that the tests routinely used for monitoring a pregnancy, for instance, ultrasound, also reveal the sex of the foetus. It has become a crime to give parents this information, but if a doctor does so, and the woman has an abortion in another clinic, the link between the two is impossible to trace. Government initiatives to address what has come to be called the 'skewed sex ratio' have thus increasingly taken forms that threaten to restrict access to abortion itself. Recently, in 2011, Indian feminists protested strongly at a statement made in the Maharashtra Legislative Assembly that 'female foeticide' should be treated as murder. There were a hundred signatories (including me) to a letter to the Speaker of the Assembly that said in part:

First of all, abortion should not be referred to as 'foeticide', which has anti-abortion implications that we reject, for we believe that all women have the right to decide when and whether to bear and give birth to children. Making sex-selective abortions (wrongly referred to as 'female foeticide') a murder charge will only increase illegal abortions and also make access to safe abortion difficult for women, who already do not have many choices regarding their own reproductive rights. Safe and legal abortion is a woman's right. Abortion is legal in India. The MTP Act, 1971 spells out the conditions under which it can be carried out.

Sex-selective abortion however, amounts to discrimination against a particular sex, in most cases, the female sex. Sex selection in favour of the boy child is a symptom of devaluation of female lives.

It is important to remember that those who want to use abortion for elimination of the female foetus have to first determine the sex of the child. Rightly, it is this process of pre-natal selection which is a crime, and it is being regulated and monitored through the PCPNDT Act.

Unless we are able to deal with all those social and economic factors that are going into the culture of son-preference and daughter-aversion, the child sex ratio will go on plummeting. But the solution is not to curb the legal right to abortion. Rather the PCPNDT Act should be enforced, and clinics that offer pre-natal sex testing weeded out . . .

Checking pre-natal sex selection requires the proper implementation of the PCPNDT Act and monitoring of sex-selective procedures by the government, and cannot be achieved by introducing such draconian measures that curb women's right to safe and legal abortion.

This letter reflects the feminist position on sex-selective abortion in India today, and marks key shifts that have taken place during the last two decades or so. 'Female foeticide', for instance, was a term that many of us used earlier. But gradually, through internal debate, we came to understanding that 'foeticide' is an emotive word, suggesting the 'murder' of the foetus who is already a separate person, and is widely used by the anti-abortion Christian right-wing in the US. The alternative term 'abortion of a pregnancy', prioritizes the pregnant woman as the implicit subject. However, in media reports, as well as in government statements, 'foeticide' (often without even the qualifying term 'female') has come to replace 'abortion' in the context of sex-selective abortion in India.

The monitoring of sex-determination tests is one thing, but it is quite another to monitor abortions themselves. Whatever the limitations of the former, the dangers of the latter are far greater. One of the measures undertaken under Renuka Chowdhury as Minister for Women and Child Development made it mandatory to register all pregnancies and to monitor abortions. A pilot project has been implemented in ten blocks with a high malnutrition rate and a skewed sex ratio. Abortions will be permitted only for 'valid and acceptable reasons' (Chauhan 2007).

But what constitutes a valid reason for abortion, and who decides? Most women in India have no control over the conditions in which they have sex and often, abortion becomes the only form of birth control. Women also have abortions because of the stigma of illegitimacy, or because they cannot afford another child, or because they are at a stage in their careers or their lives where they cannot take on the responsibility for yet another human life. Will the government officials monitoring abortions have the right to determine which is a valid reason for abortion and which is not?

This is where we come to some very difficult issues that must be addressed. First, it seems to me we cannot hold simultaneously that abortion involves the right of women to control their bodies, but that women must be restricted by law from choosing specifically to abort female foetuses. We seem to be counterposing the rights of (future) women to be born against the rights of (present) women to have control over their bodies. It is true that many women in India go in for sex-selective abortion under pressure from their husbands' families—it is not a 'choice' they make willingly. But is abortion ever a positive choice? Decisions to abort are almost always shaped by factors like those outlined above— illegitimacy, lack of social facilities for child care that place a disproportionate burden on women, economic constraints, and so on—and they are no more reflective of a woman's autonomy than her decision to abort a foetus because it is female. Nor are such decisions less determined by the constraints of a patriarchal society and a family structure based on the sexual division of labour. So why is abortion in all these other circumstances legitimate but not the abortion of female foetuses?

Second, what is our position on using pre-natal tests to detect 'foetal abnormality', a currently legal option? If we consider this valid, we are accepting a hierarchy of human beings based on physical characteristics, the lower levels of which do not have the right to be born. But then, this reasoning can be extended to other categories, such as females. One feminist response to this dilemma is to argue that since women would have the sole responsibility of looking after such children, they should have the option of whether to bear them or not. But an identical argument can be made about female children—that because the social pressure to bear male children falls entirely on the woman, she should have the right to abort a female foetus.

The painful question is this: As feminists, can we insist that individual women should have to deal with the consequences of giving birth to every kind of foetus, and that abortion should be permitted only if you know nothing about the foetus you are aborting? Can we hold the lives of existing women to ransom in order that the rights of abstract categories—'women', 'the disabled'—can be protected? Surely one can stand for the rights of existing women and people with disability while recognizing the rights of women to decide when, how and to whom to give birth?

I use the term dilemma for such instances precisely because an easy resolution of the ethical issues involved is impossible.[5] To assume that either the pro-abortion or the anti-abortion position, devoid of context, is feminist or anti-feminist in itself, is clearly ill-founded. The pregnant body, after all, is not two individuals with equal rights, it is a unique entity that cannot be addressed in the language of individualism—a life within a life, one life dependent on the other. Children are seen in the abstract as national resources but concretely, under the present sexual division of labour, must be taken care of on a day-to-day, minute-to-minute basis by their mothers. Under such circumstances, I think the host body of the mother acquires the right to decide its fate. This is why the access to safe and legal abortion should not be defended as a right of privacy. Although it is a decision taken by individual women, that decision is shaped and driven by public and social arrangements and limitations—indeed, by a collective failure of social responsibility.

There can be no quick fix for the selective abortion of female foetuses. The practice reflects the fundamental devaluing of women, which will have to be tackled in other ways, through consistent feminist politics. Such politics would have to confront marriage itself and more importantly, question the necessary framing of motherhood within discourses of hetero-patriarchal legitimacy.[6]

An ideal feminist world would not be one in which abortions were free and common, but one in which women would have greater control over pregnancy, and in which the circumstances that make pregnancies unwanted, would have been transformed. Until then, in a hugely imperfect, unfair and sexist world, I believe feminists must defend women's access to legal and safe abortions, whenever they decide to have them, whatever the reason for their decision.

This section has addressed debates among feminists that arise from complicated notions of 'agency'—women make choices, but they do not make them in circumstances of their own making. Often, women choose options that go counter to normative feminist values. What we face here is the contradiction between two core beliefs of feminism. One, the belief in the autonomy of women and their ability to act as willing agents; two, the simultaneous belief in the hegemony of dominant power-laden values that constrain the 'freedom to choose'. That is, the values that 'we' consider to be desirable are not the dominant ones in society and therefore, the freedom to choose most often simply reasserts existing dominant values which, from our point of view, are deeply problematic. Thus, a woman may choose to abort a foetus because it is female, or to acquiesce to a marriage in which her natal family will be bankrupted by dowry requirements, or to participate in a beauty contest, or take up sex work as a livelihood option. What operates here may not be 'free will' in the feminist sense but, at the same time, we cannot simply characterize it as *lack* of free will. We need to face up to this troubling recognition in our politics.

What other option do we feminists have but to treat these choices with respect, work towards changing the circumstances that shape them, continue to engage in dialogue and above all, always be open to the destabilization of our own norms?

CONCLUSION

This book has outlined a particular feminist perspective which is of course, my own position, but it is by no means an individual's opinion alone, arising in isolation. Rather, it is a voice emerging in conversation with existing strands of feminist theory and practice, and draws on a vast field of knowledge and politics outlined by feminists everywhere, over the years. At the same time, it is a perspective that runs counter to much normative feminist wisdom, and should not be seen as *the* feminist position on anything.*

This concluding chapter will touch briefly on some themes critical for feminism, which have not been raised so far.

'WOMEN'S EMPOWERMENT'

The general acceptability of the word 'gender' in the corridors of state power in India since the 1990s has been evident— a process in which the term has been domesticated into a synonym for 'women', that is, women as they are formed in patriarchal society. While in feminist vocabulary, the term 'gender' is meant to destabilize the idea of 'women', within the vocabulary of administration and state policy, 'gender' acquires quite another meaning. The common notion of

---

* Any reader of this book should know by now, of course, that there is no such thing as 'the feminist position' on anything!

'engendering' development, for instance, is about using women to regulate development. Thus, the National Policy for the Empowerment of Women (2001) states, as one of its objectives, 'mainstreaming a gender perspective in the development process.' This is explained as the ensuring of 'mainstreaming of women's perspectives in all development processes, as catalysts, participants and recipients. Wherever there are gaps in policies and programmes, women-specific interventions would be undertaken to bridge these.'[1] The complete interchangeability of 'gender' and 'women' here is striking.

The development process undertaken by the Indian State is ecologically unsustainable; it further marginalizes already- deprived communities and, since the late 1990s, involves the State acquiring agricultural lands from peasants cheaply and invariably by force, to be handed over to corporations to develop Special Economic Zones (Menon and Nigam 2007). Mainstreaming gender or adding a 'gender component' to development programmes planned within this agenda cannot possibly be a feminist goal. Essentially, this means using women's specific skills and experience produced by their location within patriarchal society (that is, precisely by the sexual division of labour), to make development programmes successful. Thus, women run households and are responsible with money, hence 'gender'-linked micro credit schemes; rural and tribal women are responsible with natural resources, so key roles for them in Joint Forest Management programmes. There is much talk of 'gender equity' without ever addressing the sexual division of labour.

Making gender a component of development depoliticizes feminist critique of patriarchy as well as feminist critiques of 'development' and of corporate globalization. Feminism is harmlessly transformed by this process into 'women's empowerment', an ally of the state project of building capitalism, essentially 'empowering' women to act as agents within the overall development agenda of the State. It is not surprising then, that NGOs which work with the government have noted that government officials make it clear that they prefer the word *stri sashaktikaran* (women's empowerment) to *narivad* (feminism).

The depoliticization (and feminization) of development discourse into 'development altruism' is also noted by a study from Kerala which suggests that the empowerment of women and the greater emphasis on women in development programmes are explicitly linked to the understanding of women as the altruistic, self-sacrificing and apolitical centres of the patriarchal family (Devika and Thampi 2010).

Of course, government programmes, despite themselves, can produce new solidarities among women drawn into them, and radicalize women hitherto unexposed to public activity. As we saw earlier, much of the political activity around sexuality has been produced by and around government-funded initiatives to control HIV/AIDS. Another striking example of this possibility is the woman who is the heroic face of feminist struggles against rape today, Bhanwari Devi. Her rape by upper-caste men of her village was in retaliation for nothing more radical than her active role in a government programme to stop child marriage. The women's movement and other democratic forces in the country rallied round her and the Vishakha guidelines on sexual harassment at the workplace by the Supreme Court were issued on an intervention inspired by her experience. Thus, government programmes do produce spaces for women to participate legitimately and actively in the public realm, and the effects of such participation can neither be accurately predicted nor strictly controlled.

Nevertheless, feminist politics needs to be very suspicious of the domestication of gender through state policy and the spurious clarity offered by government policies on 'women' and 'women's empowerment'. This clarity comes at the cost of solidifying existing patriarchal structures and cultures.

WOMEN'S MOVEMENTS IN INDIA

What constitutes 'women's movements' in India today? In the 1980s, the self-defined 'autonomous' women's movement emerged, that is, autonomous of the patriarchal control of left-wing political parties. The first national-level autonomous women's conferences were thus attended by non-funded, non-party, explicitly feminist groups. Over the 1990s, however, very few of these survived as non-funded organizations, and the Seventh National Conference of Autonomous Women's Movements in 2006 was almost entirely attended by funded NGOs. It is also important to note that many 'non'-governmental organizations receive funding from the government for specific projects, and any NGO doing a project related to 'gender' can attend the autonomous women's conferences. Thus, the only groups that are finally excluded from the umbrella of 'autonomous' women's organizations are women's wings of left-wing parties, which seems to many feminists (including me) to be a strange paradox.

Nevertheless, the sum total of interventions separately and sometimes together, by women of left-wing parties, feminist and HIV/AIDS-related NGOs, non-funded feminist and queer groups and individuals, democratic rights groups, feminist women's studies research institutes and university programmes (though not all women's studies programmes are feminist)—all these produce a distinctive feminist space in the Indian public sphere, marked as much by dissension as by agreement on different issues. The level and the intensity of the engagement and its effectiveness differ as between a 'national'-level English public to Hindi and other language publics and regions of India, each of which must be studied in its specificity. It must be clear that my focus is on the English public, though I have drawn occasionally on debates in Hindi.

SOUTH ASIAN FEMINISMS[2]

Conceptualizing South Asia as a region is a complex task, and it seems less tendentious here to remain within the framework set by current national borders, although these borders are colonial constructions for the most part. 'South' Asia has long histories of trade and cultural interchange with North Africa, West Asia and China, and the borders of the nation states of South Asia are porous for the thousands of people crossing them every day, illegally for the most part, in search of work or safety. These borders are also crossed in everyday, undramatic ways, not as conscious gestures, or in a grand and crisis-laden move, but simply because many human activities—animal herding, cultivation—simply do not adjust to modern national boundaries.

The other aspect of 'South Asia' is that the perspective changes depending on location. For those situated in Pakistan, Bangladesh or India, anti-colonial struggles and postcolonial nation-making seem to be the point of departure. This trajectory, however, has little resonance for feminists in Nepal who, in the last decade in particular, have been engaging seriously with their relationship to the Maoist movement. The Partition of the subcontinent in 1947 has had enormous significance for India, Pakistan and Bangladesh, but Sri Lanka and Nepal have other histories of national and ethnic divisions to deal with. The post-Partition history of Bangladesh and Pakistan, with the violent bitter history of the birth of Bangladesh, has produced its own trajectory of conversations among feminists in both countries, in an effort to write another history.

Relationships among these nation states are, of course, unequal and contested; they are further complicated by geopolitical developments and the differential effects of globalization and imperialist expansion on each country. It is within this variegated terrain that feminist struggles and concepts have shaped themselves and engaged with various formations of power. South Asia and hence, South Asian feminisms, cannot be held within an easily identifiable or singular framework but nevertheless, there is much in common among them.

What singularly marks this region, in fact, is the sheer presence of feminist activism throughout the past century.

Of course, we can go back further in time historically; but even if we just concentrate on the latter half of the twentieth century, the energy and the volume of work that have marked women's activism is notable. Feminist activism has engaged with religious fundamentalisms, state repression, sexual violence and livelihood issues, while women have been visibly active in all the political movements in this volatile region. Cross-border solidarities and conversations defying dominant trends of nationalist politics are a significant feature of feminist activism and scholarship in South Asia. As a line of poetry in Hindustani by Kamla Bhasin puts it,

> Main sarhad pe khadi diwaar nahin,
> Us diwaar pe padi daraar hoon.
> (I am not the wall that stands at the border,
> I am the fissure in that wall.)

AN OUTSIDE TO PATRIARCHY

Narivad, behna, dheere dheere aayi! Feminism, sister, comes slowly, slowly, sings the Delhi-based feminist group Saheli, which has remained stubbornly non-funded since its birth in 1981, when the wave of autonomous women's groups began. It's a satirical song, sung with energy and good humour, making fun of all our anxieties and quarrels — labels of funded feminism and government co-opted feminism, fear of the L word* among some old guard lefty feminists,

---

* Lesbian!

the mad confusions arising from relentlessly collective functioning and the refusal to lead or be led.

If one thinks of social order as a series of overlapping structures, then one can see that these structures have to be assembled through a variety of interventions. Even those upon whom the order is the harshest need to put in the daily hard work involved in keeping it all together. The assembling is thus continuous and works simultaneously on different parts of an already existing field; so, the assembled field is heterogeneous and layered. As every one of us participates in this assembling, either consciously building or refusing to build our parts of different structures; or simply living in certain ways that permit or do not permit structures to come together—what happens is that structures never really get to close their gates with a satisfactory click. Their borders are porous, the social order fragile, and every structure is constantly destabilized by another outside it. Like any other structure of power then, patriarchy too has an outside, which is what makes possible the different kinds of recalcitrance that constantly undermine it.*

Feminism is not about that moment of final triumph, but about the gradual transformation of the social field so decisively that old markers shift forever. This shift is what enables many young women today to say, 'I believe in equal rights for women, but I'm not a (shudder!) feminist'. Feminist struggles have made much that they fought for yesterday, the baseline beyond challenge today. In effect,

---

* I guess that's the academic way of saying naarivaad behna, dheere dheere aayi!

those privileged young women who float through their empowered lives in the wake of over a century of feminist struggles are simply disowning their own heritage. But they are not the last word, are they? From that very same social class, after all, we saw also the militant impatience of the young women who organized Slut Walk, and those who staged flash mobs against sexual harassment on Delhi's Metro.[3] And as we have seen throughout this account, there are innumerable new energies from different class and caste positions transforming the feminist field, new contestations of patriarchy, as well as contestations of normative feminism.

It comes slowly, slowly, feminism does. But it just keeps on coming!

NOTES

INTRODUCTION

1. From an on-line *Nude Make-up Tutorial.*

FAMILY

1. Harvinder Kaur vs Harmander Singh Choudhry, AIR 1984 Delhi 66. This case involved a husband seeking 'restitution of conjugal rights' which would have forced the wife to cohabit with him, and the wife claiming that the provision of restitution of conjugal rights violated fundamental rights Articles 14 (equality before law and equal protection of law) and 21 (protection of life and personal liberty), guaranteed to every citizen.
2. For some tragic accounts from Delhi of treachery and betrayal by parents of their own children who fall in love with the wrong people, and the kinds of physical violence unleashed on rebellious couples by their own families, see Perveez Mody (2008).
3. An important feminist study of domestic servants in India is by Raka Ray and Seemin Qayum (2009). See also, on male domestic servants, Radhika Chopra (2006).
4. Virilocality is also a feature of some matrilineal societies, but the impact in that case is different, for the woman inherits natal property, and may return later in life to build a home

near her parents and live there with her husband and children. See Janaki Abraham (2011).

5. In other cases where the husband has objected, court rulings have prevented divorced women from using their married name.

6. 'Upper Caste Woman's Marriage to Dalit no ticket for Poll Quota', *The Tribune*, Chandigarh, 1 February 2005; 'Child will inherit only father's caste: court', *The Hindu*, New Delhi, 29 January 2005

7. The three judges were Chief Justice R.C. Lahoti and Justices G.P. Mathur and P.K. Balsubramanyam. Later, in 2005, a seven-judge Bench, including these three, abolished caste-based reservation in private, unaided professional colleges. Interestingly, in the same judgment the Bench allowed a quota for Non-Resident Indians. See J. Venkatesan, 'No quota in unaided private colleges', *The Hindu*, 13 August 2005.

8. *Kanyadan*, giving away a daughter in marriage, is seen as a religious duty in Hinduism, and is often performed for poor girls by private individuals or organizations.

9. Lakshmi (1989), cited in Basu (2009).

10. Respondent to Rita Kothari (2009:166)

11. For a detailed account, see Nivedita Menon (forthcoming).

BODY

1. English translation in A.K. Ramanujan (1973: 29, 110).

2. Ibid.,129.

3. Bindu Menon in a comment on my post, 'The Disappearing Body and Feminist Thought' on the blog kafila. http://kafila.org/2011/02/18/the-disappearing-body-and-feminist-thought/ The works referred to by Bindu Menon are Sreekumar (2006) and Madathil (2010).

4. This letter appeared in *The Asian Age* (Delhi) sometime in the late 1990s. By now, plastic surgery advertisements routinely

offer both breast augmentation for women as well as breast reduction for gynaecomastia.

5. Thanks to Sadanand Menon for a graphic account!
6. There is a large body of scholarship but, for instance, for Hinduism, see Gatwood (1985), and Humes and McDermot (2009); for Christianity, Ruether (1994).
7. Thanks to Chayanika Shah for a discussion on this.
8. A genetic disorder of the connective tissue. People with Marfan's tend to be unusually tall, with long limbs and long, thin fingers.
9. For an English translation of this story, see J. Devika (2007).

DESIRE

1. See Ann Laura Stoler (2002) for a dazzling overview of this literature.
2. Self description in invitation to a public event.
3. However, some activists told reporters they would have preferred the new category to be T for 'transgender', since *hijras* represent only one part of the transgender population. 'Third sex finds a place on Indian passport forms' Infochange Human Rights. See http://www.infochangeindia.org/HumanItop.jsp?section_idv=13#3801
   See also, Shibu Thomas 'Column for eunuchs in passport form', *Midday*, 9 March 2005, p.1.
4. The provisions of Section 377 IPC will continue to govern non-consensual penile non-vaginal sex and penile non-vaginal sex involving minors.

SEXUAL VIOLENCE

1. Reported in *The Hindu*, 9 February 2008.
2. Reported in *The Indian Express*, 9 February 2008. For an open letter of protest to these officials by the organization, Stree Mukti, see http://www.countercurrents.org/streemukti280208.htm

3. State of Punjab v Major Singh, 1967.
4. http://www.independent.co.uk/news/world/asia/british-woman-tells-of-humiliation-by-indian-court-1790194.html
5. http://articles.timesofindia.indiatimes.com/2009-07-12/india/28161957_1_woman-army-officer-flying-officer-anjali-gupta-general-cour
6. http://articles.timesofindia.indiatimes.com/2011-09-11/india/30141416_1_anjali-gupta-bhopal-cashiered
7. 'Rape convict cracks UPSC', *The Times of India*, 11 February 2009.
8. An application under the Right to Information (RTI) Act that requires government and affiliated institutions to furnish information to the public.
9. A UK- based support group for women who have suffered sexual assault.
10. http://www.womenagainstrape.net/inthemedia/women-question-unusual-zeal-pursuing-julian-assang
11. Angry Malay woman, 'What Malaysians can do to end rape' on Kakak Killjoy, feminist webzine.
12. http://www.indianexpress.com/news/to-slam-mamata-cpm-mp-cites-us-prostitutes/780525/
13. http://www.indianexpress.com/news/god-of-garbeta-lands-behind-bars/830898/0
14. Archana Verma's article is in Hindi. The translation here, of relevant passages is mine. A translation in English by Ruth Vanita and Simona Sawhney of the entire article is available (2010).
15. For an account of Indian democracy since 1989 see Menon and Nigam (2007).

FEMINISTS AND 'WOMEN'

1. A provision under the Muslim Personal Law that enables Muslim men to divorce unilaterally by uttering the word *talaq* three times.

2. This was a case of a Hindu married man converting to Islam in order to marry for the second time. Flavia Agnes points out that the judgment focused entirely on the Muslim Personal Law, avoiding entirely the issue of bigamy by Hindu men, thus deliberately and wrongly assuming that breach of monogamy is possible for Hindu men only by conversion to Islam.

3. The Mumbai-based feminist organization, Majlis, brought this judgment to the attention of feminists in India through a campaign to protect the rights of 'women in a marriage-like relationship with men who are already married'.

4. http://www.swissinfo.ch/eng/Muslim_angered_by_unjust_headscarf_sport_ban.html?cid=63872

5. Other Backward Castes, the 'socially and educationally backward castes' recognized by government policy.

6. Some terms that need explanation here arise from the long history of militant politics of caste in Tamil Nadu. The movement against Brahmin hegemony was led by 'non-Brahmins' or Dravidians (Shudras, those occupying the fourth position in the caste hierarchy). The goal of this movement was to build a larger unity of non-Brahmins/Dravidians with the 'fifth caste', the Dalits. While it has been a powerful and effective struggle, the current power wielded by Dravidians in Tamil society has led to a gradual alienation of Dalits from this alliance.

7. These have taken place most recently in the debates around the 'Ambedkar cartoon controversy' on the blogs Round Table India, Kafila and Savari. Feminist sociologist Sharmila Rege has worked consistently over decades to make visible both caste oppression and caste privilege, and has recently brought together autobiographical accounts of Dalit Women in *Writing Caste/Writing Gender* (2006).

VICTIMS OR AGENTS?

1. *Capital*, vol. 1, chap. 1, sec. 4.
2. *Capital*, vol. 1, chap. 2.
3. Cited by McElroy, nd.
4. *Manushi*, editorial, No. 37, 1986.
5. Feminist engagement with the moral dilemmas involved in aborting foetuses judged to be 'disabled' is extremely complex. See Menon (2004) for an account.
6. The inner subjectivities of mothers of daughters in a culture of son-preference, has been creatively explored by feminist psychologist Rachana Johri (2001, 2010)

CONCLUSION

1. http://wcd.nic.in/empwomen.htm
2. This section draws extensively on an Introduction written jointly with Firdous Azim and Dina M. Siddiqui, to a special issue of *Feminist Review* that we edited, 'South Asian Feminisms. Negotiating New Terrains' (No. 91, 2009). Interested readers will find in this issue, papers by feminists from Nepal, Pakistan, Sri Lanka, Bangladesh and India on different aspects of politics, culture and the economy as well as feminist fiction and poetry from the region.
3. http://www.youtube.com/watch?v=KD3y3nd90I0

BIBLIOGRAPHY

OF GENERAL INTEREST

Chaudhuri, Maitrayee. Ed. 2005. *Feminism in India*. Delhi: Kali for Women.

Geetha, V. 2002. *Gender*. Kolkata: Stree.

————2007. *Patriarchy*. Kolkata: Stree.

John, Mary. Ed. 2008. *Women's Studies in India: A Reader*. Delhi: Penguin.

Menon, Nivedita. 1999. *Gender and Politics in India*. Delhi: Oxford University Press.

Sangari, Kumkum, and Sudesh Vaid. Eds. 1990. *Recasting Women: Essays in Indian Colonial History*. New Brunswick: Rutgers University Press; Delhi: Kali for Women.

WORKS CITED IN THE TEXT

Abraham, Janaki. 2011. '"Why Did You Send Me Like This?": Marriage, Matriliny and the "Providing Husband" in North Kerala, India'. *Asian Journal of Women's Studies*, 17(2).

Adams, Cecil. 2008. 'Was Pink Originally the Color for Boys and Blue for Girls?' *The Straight Dope*. http://www.straightdope. com/columns/read/2831/was-pink-originally-the-color-for-boys-and-blue-for-girls

AFP (Agence France-Presse). 2011. 'Indian Brides Told to Put Down Their Mobile Phones'. *Asia One News*, 9 May.

Agnes, Flavia. 1992. 'Protecting Women against Violence? Review of a Decade of Legislation 1980–89'. *Economic & Political Weekly*, 25 April.

————1994. 'Women's Movement within a Secular Framework: Redefining the Agenda'. *Economic & Political Weekly*, 29(19).

————1999. *Law and Gender Equality: The Politics of Women's Rights in India.* Delhi: Oxford University Press.

————2006. 'The Bar Dancer and the Trafficked Migrant: Globalisation and Subaltern Existence'. Inaugural Lecture delivered at the 'Fourth Annual Winter Course on Forced Migration'. Organized by Mahanirban Calcutta Research Group. December. Available at http://www.majlisbombay.org/pdfs/03.%20%20Link%20to%20bar%20dancers(3).pdf

Amadiume, Ifi. 1987. *Male Daughters, Female Husbands: Gender and Sex in an African Society.* London: Zed Books.

Ambedkar, B.R. 1936. 'Annihilation of Caste'. *B.R. Ambedkar's Writings and Speeches*, vol. 1. Compiled by Vasant Moon, Education Department, Government of Maharashtra, Mumbai, 1979.

Anand, Utkarsh. 2009. 'Bride's Father in the Dock as City Court Says Giving Dowry Is Also an Offence'. *The Indian Express*, 11 August.

Anandhi, S., J. Jeyaranjan and Rajan Krishnan. 2002. 'Work, Caste and Competing Masculinities: Notes from a Tamil Village'. *Economic & Political Weekly*, 26 October.

Arunima, G. 2003. *There Comes Papa: Colonialism and the Transformation of Matriliny in Kerala, Malabar c.1850–1940.* Hyderabad: Orient Longman.

Azim, Firdous, Nivedita Menon and Dina M. Siddiqui. Eds. 2009. 'Introduction'. *Feminist Review*, 91.

Basu, Srimati. 2009. 'Legacies of the Dowry Prohibition Act in India'. *Dowry: Bridging the Gap between Theory and Practice*. Eds. Tamsin Bradley, Emma Tomalin and Mangala Subramaniam. Delhi: Women Unlimited.

Baxi, Pratiksha. 2011. 'In Support of the Besharmi Morcha/ Slutwalk'. *OneWorld South Asia*. http://southasia.oneworld. net/opinioncomment/supporting-besharmi-morcha-2018slutwalk2019

Belkin, Lisa. 2009. 'Boycotting Pink Toys for Girls'. *The New York Times*, 22 December.

Bhattacharya, Rimli. 2003. 'The Nautee in "the Second City of the Empire"'. *The Indian Economic and Social History Review*, 40(2).

Bijapurkar, Rama. 2011. 'Maid to Order. Ladies, Some HR Management Tips for Your Home'. *The Indian Express, The Eye*, 27 March–2 April.

Boylan, Jennifer Finney. 2008. 'The XY Games'. *The New York Times*, 3 August.

Butalia, Urvashi. 2011. 'Mona's Story'. *Granta 115: The F Word*, 114, Spring.

Butler, Judith. 1990. *Gender Trouble*. New York, London: Routledge.

———1993. *Bodies that Matter*. New York, London: Routledge.

Buzuvis, Erin. 2010. 'Caster Semenya and the Myth of a Level Playing Field'. *The Modern American*, 6(2).

Chakravarti, Uma. 1983. 'Rape, Class and the State' in PUCL (People's Union of Civil Liberties) Bulletin. September. http:// www.pucl.org/from-archives/Gender/rape-class.htm

Chandralekha. 1992. 'Who Are These Age-Old Female Figures?' *The Economic Times*, 8 March.

Chauhan, Chetan. 2007. 'Govt to Monitor Pregnancies, Abortions'. *Hindustan Times*, 13 July.

Chopra, Radhika. 2003. 'From Violence to Supportive Practice. Family, Gender and Masculinities'. *Economic & Political Weekly*, 26 April.

———2007. 'Invisible Men: Masculinity, Sexuality, and Male Domestic Labor'. *Men and Masculinities*, 9(2).

Chowdhry, Prem. 2004. 'Caste Panchayats and the Policing of Marriage in Haryana: Enforcing Kinship and Territorial Exogamy'. *Contributions to Indian Sociology* (n.s.), 38(1, 2).

De Alwis, Malathi. 1997. 'Motherhood as a Space of Protest: Women's Political Participation in Contemporary Sri Lanka'. *Appropriating Gender: Women's Activism and the Politicization of Religion in South Asia*. Eds Amrita Basu and Patricia Jeffrey. London, New York: Routledge; Delhi: Kali for Women.

Deshpande, Swati. 2011. 'Divorcees Can Retain Surnames'. *The Times of India*, 3 October.

Devika, J. 2007. 'On the Far Side of Memory'. *Sexualities*. Ed. Nivedita Menon. Delhi: Women Unlimited. (English translation of Lalitambika Antharjanam's Malayalam short story 'Ormayude Appuratthu' in the collection *Agnipushpangal*. Kottayam: Sahitya Pravartaka Cooperative Society. 1960.)

Devika, J., and Binitha Thampi. 2010. 'Mobility towards Work and Politics for Women in Kerala: A View from the Histories of Gender and Space.' *Modern Asian Studies*, 45(5).

Fausto-Sterling, Anne. 2002. 'The Five Sexes: Why Male and Female Are Not Enough'. *Sexuality and Gender*. Eds. Christine L. Williams and Arlene Stein. Oxford: Blackwell.

Gandhi, Nandita, and Nandita Shah. 1992. *The Issues at Stake*. New Delhi: Kali for Women.

Gatwood, Lynn E. 1985. *Devi and the Spouse Goddess: Women, Sexuality, and Marriages in India*. Riverdale: Riverdale Co.

Ghai, Anita. 2002. 'Disabled Women: An Excluded Agenda of Indian Feminism'. *Hypatia*, 17(3), Summer.

Ghatwai, Milind. 2009. "'Virginity' Row: MP Sets Scheme Selection Rules". *The Indian Express*, 5 September.

Ghosh, Shohini. 1999. 'The Troubled Existence of Sex and Sexuality: Feminists Engage with Censorship'. *Image Journeys: Audio-Visual Media and Cultural Change in India*. Eds. Christiane Brosius and Melissa Butcher. New Delhi: Sage.

Gilligan, Carol. 1982. *In a Different Voice: Psychological Theory and Women's Development*. Cambridge: Harvard University Press.

Gunu, K. 2010. 'Supreme Court of India Bats for Women's Work'. http://www.worldpulse.com/node/23298

Gupta, Alok. 2005. 'Englishpur Ki Kothi. Class Dynamics in the Queer Movement in India'. *Because I Have a Voice: Queer Politics in India*. Eds. Arvind Narrain and Gautam Bhan Narrain. Delhi: Yoda Press.

Gupta, Alok, and Arvind Narrain. 2010. Introduction to *Law like Love*. Delhi: Yoda Press.

Haksar, Nandita.1999. 'Human Rights Layering: A Feminist Perspective'. *Engendering Law: Essays in Honour of Lotika Sarkar*. Eds. Amita Dhanda and Archana Parasher. Lucknow: Eastern Book Company, 1999.

Halder, Baby. 2006. *A Life Less Ordinary*. Delhi: Zubaan Books.

Halley, Janet. 2011. Presentation at MISR Contemporary Debates Workshop: Gender and the Public Sphere. http://misr.mak. ac.ug/uploads/Halley%20Presentation.pdf

Halley, Janet, Prabha Kotiswaran, Hila Shamir and Chantal Thomas. 2006. 'From the International to the Local in Feminist Legal Responses to Rape, Prostitution/Sex Work, and Sex Trafficking: Four Studies in Contemporary Governance Feminism'. *Harvard Journal of Law and Gender*, 29.

Hansen, Kathryn. 1999. 'Making Women Visible: Gender and Race Cross-Dressing in the Parsi Theatre'. *Theatre Journal*, 51(2).

Humes, Cynthia Ann, and Rachel Fell McDermott. Eds. 2009. *Breaking Boundaries with the Goddess*. Delhi: Manohar.

Hunasavadi, Srikanth. 2011. 'Daily Working Hours for Women All Set to Go Up in Karnataka'. 23 February. http://www.dnaindia. com/bangalore/report_daily-working-hours-for-women-all-set-to-go-up-in-karnataka_1511640

Jaggar, Alison M. 1983. *Feminist Politics and Human Nature.* Sussex: Harvester Press.

Jebaraj, Priscilla. 2011. 'Turning Baby Girls into Boys? The Scoop That Wasn't'. *The Hindu,* 20 July.

Jesani, Amar, and Aditi Iyer. 1993. 'Women and Abortion'. *Economic & Political Weekly,* 27 November.

Johri, Rachana. 2001. 'Resisting the Cultural Construction of Mothering Daughters: Narratives from Mothers with Married Daughters'. Unpublished paper. Presented at University of Queensland, Brisbane, Australia.

————2010. 'Mothering from the Margins: The Mother–Daughter Relationship in a Culture of Son-Preference'. *Attachment: Expanding the Cultural Constructions.* Eds. Phyllis Erdman and Kok-Mun Ng. New York: Routledge, Taylor and Francis.

Kakar, Sudhir. 1989. *Intimate relations: Exploring Indian Sexuality.* Delhi: Penguin.

Kalra, Nonita. 2011. 'Do You Deserve a Good Maid?' *The Indian Express,* 1 May.

Kapur, Anuradha. 1993. 'Deity to Crusader: The Changing Iconography of Ram'. *Hindus and Others: The Question of Identity in India Today.* Ed. Gyanendra Pandey. New Delhi: Viking.

Kapur, Ratna. 2005. *Erotic Justice: Law and the New Politics of Postcolonialism.* Delhi: Permanent Black.

Kaur, Ravinder. 2008. 'Dispensable Daughters and Bachelor Sons: Sex Discrimination in North India'. *Economic & Political Weekly,* 26 July.

Kessler, Suzanne J. 1990. 'The Medical Construction of Gender:

Case Management of Intersexed Infants'. *Signs: Journal of Women in Culture and Society*, Autumn.

Kishwar, Madhu. 1994. 'Codified Hindu Law: Myth and Reality'. *Economic & Political Weekly*, 13 August.

Kodoth, Praveena. 2001. 'Courting Legitimacy or Delegitimizing Custom? Sexuality, Sambandham and Marriage Reform in Late-Nineteenth Century Malabar'. *Modern Asian Studies*, 35(2).

Kothari, Rita. 2009. *The Burden of Refuge*. Hyderabad: Orient BlackSwan.

Kotiswaran, Prabha. 2011. *Dangerous Sex, Invisible Labor: Sex Work and the Law in India*. New Jersey: Princeton University Press.

Krishna Raj, Maithreyi. 1990. 'Women's Work in the Indian Census'. *Economic & Political Weekly*, 1–8 December.

Krishna Raj, Maithreyi, and Vibhuti Patel. 1982. 'Women's Liberation and the Political Economy of Housework: An Indian Perspective'. *Women's Studies International*, 2, July.

Kumar, Radha. 1993. *The History of Doing*. Delhi: Kali for Women.

Kumar, Udaya. 1997. 'Self, Body and Inner Sense: Some Reflections on Sree Narayana Guru and Kumaran Asan'. *Studies in History*, 13(2).

Kumar, Vinoj. 2010. 'Free Sanitary Napkins: A Scam in the Making?' http://pcvinojkumar.blogspot.com/2010/02/free-sanitary-napkins-scam-in-making.html

Lakshmanan, C. 2004. 'Dalit Masculinities in Social Science Research: Revisiting a Tamil Village'. *Economic & Political Weekly*, 6 March.

Lakshmi, C.S. 1989. 'On Kidneys and Dowry'. *Economic & Political Weekly*, 28 January.

Madathil, Sajitha. 2010. *Malayalanatakasthricharithram*. Kozhikode: Mathrubhumi. (Malayalam).

Majlis. 2005. *Abuse of Power*. (Report on Bar Dancers after the Ban on Their Profession.) Mumbai: Majlis.

Martin, Emily. 1991. 'The Egg and the Sperm: How Science Has Constructed a Romance Based on Stereotypical Male–Female Roles'. *Signs: Journal of Women in Culture and Society*, 16(3).

McElroy, Wendy. 2010. 'Feminists against Women: The New Reproductive Technologies'. http://www.wendymcelroy.com/reason2.htm

Menon, Nivedita. 2004. *Recovering Subversion. Feminist Politics beyond the Law*. Delhi: Permanent Black; Champaign: University of Illinois Press.

———2011. 'Modest? Sexy? Or Just an Athlete?' On the blog Kafila. http://kafila.org/2011/04/27/modest-sexy-or-just-an-athlete/

———(forthcoming). 'Cooking Up Nature: Science in the World of Politics'. *Critical Studies in Politics*. Eds. Nivedita Menon, Aditya Nigam and Sanjay Palshikar. Hyderabad: Orient BlackSwan.

Menon, Nivedita, and Aditya Nigam. 2007. *Power and Contestation: India since 1989*. London: Zed Books; Hyderabad: Orient Longman.

Mernissi, Fatima. 1987. 'The Muslim Concept of Active Female Sexuality'. *Beyond the Veil. Male–Female Dynamics in Modern Muslim Society*. Bloomington: Indiana University Press.

Mody, Perveez. 2008. *The Intimate State: Love-Marriage and the Law in Delhi*. Oxford, New Delhi: Routledge.

Mookherjee, Nayanika. 2011. 'The Absent Piece of Skin: Gendered, Racialized and Territorial Inscriptions of Sexual Violence During Bangladesh War.' *Modern Asian Studies*. Published online 4 January 2012.

Mulvey, Laura. 1975. 'Visual Pleasure and Narrative Cinema'. *Screen*, 16(3).

Najmabadi, Afsaneh. 2005. *Women with Moustaches and Men without Beards. Gender and Sexual Anxieties of Iranian Modernity*. Berkeley, California: University of California Press.

Nandy, Ashis. 1983. *The Intimate Enemy. Loss and Recovery of Self under Colonialism.* Delhi: Oxford University Press.

Narrain, Arvind, and Gautam Bhan. Ed. 2005. *Because I Have a Voice: Queer Politics in India.* Delhi: Yoda Press.

Oudshoorn, Nelly. 1994. *Beyond the Natural Body: An Archaeology of Sex Hormones.* London, New York: Routledge.

Oyewumi, Oyeronke. 1997. *The Invention of Women: Making an African Sense of Western Gender Discourses.* Minneapolis: University of Minnesota Press.

Pande, Amrita. 2009. 'Not an "Angel", Not a "Whore": Surrogates as "Dirty" Workers in India'. *The Indian Journal of Gender Studies,* 16(2).

Parasher, Archana. 1992. *Women and Family Law Reform in India.* Delhi: Sage Publications.

Phadke, Shilpa. 2007. 'Dangerous Liaisons: Women and Men— Risk and Reputation in Mumbai'. *Economic & Political* Weekly, 28 April.

Pillai, Supriya, Meena Seshu and Meena Shivdas. 2008. 'Embracing the Rights of People in Prostitution and Sex Workers, to Address HIV and AIDS effectively'. *Gender & Development,* 16(2), 2 July.

PUCL (People's Union of Civil Liberties). 2003. *Human Rights Violations against the Transgender Community: A Study of Hijra and Kothi Sex Workers in Bangalore, India.* Karnataka: People's Union for Civil Liberties. September.

Qadeer, Imrana, and Mary E. John. 2008. 'Surrogacy Politics' at Kafila.org. http://kafila.org/2008/12/25/surrogacy-politics-imrana-qadeer-mary-e-john/ Downloaded 14 October 2011.

Ramanujan, A.K. 1973. *Speaking of Siva.* London, New York: Penguin Classics.

Ray, Raka, and Seemin Qayum. 2009. *Cultures of Servitude: Modernity, Domesticity, and Class in India.* Palo Alto: Stanford University Press.

Raymond, Janice G. 1993. *Women as Wombs: Reproductive Technologies and the Battle over Women's Freedom*. San Francisco: Harper.

Rege, Sharmila. 2006. *Writing Caste, Writing Gender*. Delhi: Zubaan.

Revathi, A., and V. Geetha. 2010. *The Truth about Me: A Hijra Life Story*. Delhi: Penguin.

Roscoe, Will. 1988. *Living the Spirit: A Gay American Indian Anthology*. New York: St Martin's Griffin.

Ruether, Rosemary Radford. 1994. 'Ecofeminism: Symbolic and Social Connections of the Oppression of Women and the Domination of Nature'. *Ecological Prospects: Scientific, Religious and Aesthetic Perspectives*. Ed. Christopher Key Chapple. Albany: State University of New York Press.

Sahni, Rohini, and V. Kalyan Shankar. 2011. *The First Pan-India Survey of Sex Workers: A Summary of Preliminary Findings*. http://sangram.org/Download/Pan-India-Survey-of-Sex-workers.pdf

Sarojini, N.B., and Dharashree Das. 2010. 'ARTs: Voices from Progressive Movements'. *Making Babies: Birth Markets and Assisted Reproductive Technologies in India*. Ed. Sandhya Srinivasan. New Delhi: Zubaan.

Scott, James. 1998. *Seeing Like a State: How Certain Schemes to Improve the Human Condition Have Failed*. New Haven: Yale University Press.

Sen, Amartya. 2006. *Identity and Violence: The Illusion of Destiny*. New York: W.W. Norton & Company.

Shah, Svati. 2003. 'Sex Work in the Global Economy'. *New Labor Forum*, 12(1), Spring.

Shanley, Laura. 2007. 'Milkmen: Fathers Who Breastfeed'. http://www.socalbirth.com/pdf/milkmen.pdf

Sharma, Garima, and Chandna Arora. 2011. 'So, What's Your Name Now, Ma'am?' *The Times of India*, 17 October.

Sharma, Jaya, and Deepika Nath. 2005. 'Through the Prism of Intersectionality: Same Sex Sexualities in India'. *Sexuality, Gender and Rights: Exploring Theory and Practice in South and Southeast Asia*. Eds. Geetanjali Misra and Radhika Chandiramani. New Delhi: Sage.

Sharma, Nandita. 2003. 'Travel Agency: A Critique of Anti-Trafficking Campaigns'. *Refuge*, 21(3), May.

Shiva, Vandana. 1988. *Staying Alive: Women, Ecology and Survival in India*. London: Zed Books; New Delhi: Women Unlimited.

Singh, Kirti. 2012. 'This Too Is Loaded against Women'. *The Times of India, The Crest Edition*.

Sinha, Chitra. 2007. 'Images of Motherhood: The Hindu Code Bill Discourse'. *Economic & Political Weekly*, 27 October.

Siwach, Sukhbir. 2011. 'Not My Son's Father'. *The Times of India*, 13 November.

Sreekumar, K. 2006. *Ochira Velukkutty*. Thrissur: Kerala Sangeetha Nataka Akademi. (Malayalam).

Steinem, Gloria. 1978. 'If Men Could Menstruate'. *Ms Magazine*, October. Available at http://www.mum.org/ifmencou.htm

Stemple, Lara. 2009. 'Male Rape and Human Rights'. http://uchastings.edu/hlj/archive/vol60/Stemple_60-HLJ-605.pdf

Stephen, Cynthia. 2009. 'Feminism or Womanism? A Personal Herstory'. Insight Young Voices Blog. http://blog.insightyv.com/?p=837

Stoler, Ann Laura. 2002. *Carnal Knowledge and Imperial Power: Race and the Intimate in Colonial Rule*. Berkeley, Los Angeles, London: University of California Press.

Susan, Nisha. 2009. 'Why We Said Pants to India's Bigots'. *The Observer*, 15 February.

Swaminathan, Nikhil. 2007. 'Strange but True: Males Can Lactate'. *Scientific American*, 6 September.

Teman, Elly. 2003. 'The Medicalization of "Nature" in the "Artificial Body": Surrogate Motherhood in Israel'. *Medical*

Anthropology Quarterly, 17(1).

Tomalin, Emma. 2009. Introduction to *Dowry: Bridging the Gap between Theory and Practice*. Eds. Tamsin Bradley, Emma Tomalin and Mangala Subramaniam. Delhi: Women Unlimited.

Truitt, Eliza. 2001. 'Athletes in Skirts'. *Slate Magazine*, 6 July. http://www.slate.com/articles/arts/culturebox/2001/07/athletes_in_skirts.html

Vance, Carole. Ed. 1984. *Pleasure and Danger: Exploring Female Sexuality*. London: Routledge and Kegan Paul.

————1992. 'More Danger, More Pleasure: A Decade after the Barnard Sexuality Conference'. Preface to *Pleasure and Danger*, 2nd ed. (1984).

Vanita, Ruth, and Saleem Kidwai. 2000. *Same-Sex Love in India: Readings from Literature and History*. New York: St Martin's Press.

Vanita, Ruth, and Simona Sawhney. 2010. 'A Grand Celebration of Feminist Discourse'. *Seminar*. (Translation of Archana Verma, 2010)

Verma, Archana. 2010. 'Stree Vimarsh Ke Mahotsav'. *Kathadesh*. (Hindi).

Vijay, Anant. 2010. 'The Chhinaal Controversy'. *FacenFacts*. http://www.facenfacts.com/NewsDetails/127/the-chhinaal-controversy.htm

Wajihuddin, Mohammed. 2011. 'Islam, Women and Feminism'. New Age Islam. http://www.newageislam.com/NewAgeIslamArticleDetail.aspx?ArticleID=4753

Waldby, Catherine. 2010. 'Rent-a-Womb Trend Is a Form of Neo-Colonialism'. Interview with Venkatesan Vembu. *Daily News and Analysis*, 24 July. http://www.dnaindia.com/india/interview_rent-a-womb-trend-is-a-form-of-neo-colonialism_1413754 Downloaded 13 October 2010.

Wolf, Naomi. 2008. 'Behind the Veil Lives a Thriving Muslim Sexuality'. *The Sunday Morning Herald*, 30 August.

ACKNOWLEDGEMENTS

Janaki Abraham, Pratiksha Baxi, Pramada Menon and Aditya Nigam read earlier drafts, and gave me invaluable inputs. So faithfully did I take their advice that it might be appropriate to say that any errors, weakness in argumentation and general stodginess that remain are entirely their responsibility.

Thanks to R. Sivapriya of Penguin and Urvashi Butalia of Zubaan for flippant email exchanges that had no meaning whatever in the larger scheme of things.

This book distils over two decades of engagement with the politics that has shaped me, and would not have been possible without the conversations, campaigns, arguments, fights, books, films, friendships, splits and solidarities that have made up my life.

Here's to feminists of every gender, everywhere, anywhere. And to those who engage seriously enough with feminism to push us, kicking and screaming, in unexpected directions.

And to those who will become feminists at some stage.

Our lives are meaningful because of one another.

INDEX